THE WIND AT MY BACK

Resilience, Grace, and Other Gifts from My Mentor, Raven Wilkinson

MISTY COPELAND

with Susan Fales-Hill

GRAND CENTRAL
PUBLISHING

NEW YORK   BOSTON

Grand Central Publishing
Hachette Book Group
1290 Avenue of the Americas, New York, NY 10104
grandcentralpublishing.com
twitter.com/grandcentralpub

First edition: November 2022

Grand Central Publishing is a division of Hachette Book Group, Inc. The Grand Central Publishing name and logo is a trademark of Hachette Book Group, Inc.

The publisher is not responsible for websites (or their content) that are not owned by the publisher.

Library of Congress Cataloging-in-Publication Data

Names: Copeland, Misty, author.
Title: The wind at my back : resilience, grace, and other gifts from my mentor, Raven Wilkinson / Misty Copeland.
Description: New York : Grand Central Publishing, [2022] | Includes index.
Identifiers: LCCN 2022026199 | ISBN 9781538753859 (hardcover) | ISBN 9781538740170 | ISBN 9781538740187 | ISBN 9781538740194 | ISBN 9781538753866 (ebook)
Subjects: LCSH: Copeland, Misty. | Wilkinson, Raven. | African American ballerinas—Biography. | African American ballerinas—Social conditions. | Ballerinas—Biography. | Ballet dancers—United States—Biography. | Ballet—United States—History—20th century. | Mentoring in the arts—United States. | Racism—United States—History—20th century.
Classification: LCC GV1785.C635 A3 2022 | DDC 792.802/80922 [B]—dc23
LC record available at https://lccn.loc.gov/2022026199

ISBNs: 9781538753859 (hardcover), 9781538753866 (ebook), 9781538740187 (signed edition), 9781538740170 (B&N.com), 9781538740194 (B&N holiday)

Printed in the United States of America

LSC-C

Printing 1, 2022

To all the incredible mentors in the world who have guided, inspired, motivated, and championed others to believe in themselves and continue the cycle of leadership. Olu, for being an incredible partner, and for your unwavering support and belief in me. To our son, Jackson, for showing me how to love and lead in a new way. And last but not least, to my mentor, Raven Wilkinson, for your enduring grace and resilience, and for showing me the importance of working toward a purpose bigger than ourselves.

CONTENTS

PROLOGUE: On the Shoulders of Giants *1*

CHAPTER 1: It All Began Tonight *11*

CHAPTER 2: A Distant Mirror *17*

CHAPTER 3: Two Women at the Crossroads *27*

CHAPTER 4: Never Give Up *47*

CHAPTER 5: Taking Flight *75*

CHAPTER 6: Dreams Deferred *99*

CHAPTER 7: Black Swans Rock *121*

CHAPTER 8: Blood, Sweat, and Swan Queens *131*

CHAPTER 9: Live by the Swan, Die by the Swan *145*

CHAPTER 10: Dreams Realized *161*

CHAPTER 11: The Bells Toll *175*

CHAPTER 12: Taking Raven's Breath Away *181*

CHAPTER 13: Transition *189*

EPILOGUE: Blackface, Racial Reckoning, and Raven's Wish *203*

ACKNOWLEDGMENTS 215

NOTES 217

INDEX 221

ON THE SHOULDERS OF GIANTS

It's only in trying and keeping going that you achieve, you can't expect that it's all going to happen for you just because you're out there pointing your toes nicely. You have to open your mind and heart, and you must believe in yourself and have faith and hope.

—RAVEN WILKINSON

On an unusually cold evening in late March, I nestled on my couch with my feet up after a long day. I caressed my belly to soothe my growing son, who was in a restless mood, kicking up a storm. With his "grands battements," he seemed eager to let me know he wanted to "get out" and see the world, and I certainly couldn't wait to meet him. I lay back, eating sunflower seeds—my favorite snack as a child had become somewhat of a comfort food now that I was an adult. As I cracked open the salty shells, I wondered if my son would enjoy them like I had with my dad. Already, I was assessing the world around me, from the smallest, most ordinary items, like my favorite snack, to the largest challenges, like the state of the justice system and the destruction of the environment, in terms of how they would affect him. Like I imagine most mothers who are expecting do, I fantasized about introducing my child to my many loves that make life beautiful: music, from Mariah Carey to Beethoven, Japanese gardens, and Marius Petipa ballets. But I also worried about the realities of bringing a Black boy into the world—exposing him to the war, racism, and inequality that are part of our current reality. I am so grateful to have an incredible partner in parenthood, my husband, Olu.

Even though our nation had made so much progress, and the reckoning in the wake of the murder of George Floyd had brought so many honest conversations to the forefront, like countless Black mothers before me, I nursed high hopes and huge fears about what the future held for my boy. Who would my son be? What would he want to become? Would he find himself one of only a handful, a "rare" and highly scrutinized few in the field he was most passionate about? Would doors be open to him, or would he have to break them down with the help of so many others who had tried before him? I couldn't help but think of my own journey to being "the first" Black female principal dancer at American Ballet Theatre. I wanted his path to be smoother, but in the pit of my stomach, I grappled with a deep anxiety that it wouldn't be.

That night, I didn't feel like reading or binge-watching a favorite series. The Senate hearings for the confirmation of Supreme Court nominee Ketanji Brown Jackson were in full swing. I wanted to witness history in the making, so I turned on C-SPAN to see what I'd missed that day.

Judge Brown Jackson sat calmly at the table, her hands neatly folded before her, maintaining her composure as questioner after questioner sought to paint her as "soft on child pornographers" in her sentencing practices, interrupting her as she attempted to answer, and distorting her record beyond recognition. She never raised her voice; she never lost her temper in a situation in which any normal human being would have been justified in exploding. I watched her in one moment literally swallow her outrage and take a breath before responding evenly and respectfully with well-reasoned facts. I believed I knew what kept her centered. As I watched her sit there stoically, taking everything that was thrown at her, I imagined she was thinking: "I'm the first. I'm in the room. Many fought for me to be here. No one said it would be easy. There are those who are determined to see me live up to every stereotype of the emotionally undisciplined angry Black woman, and I won't. This is bigger than just me."

It was the same act of will that enabled my mentor, Raven

Wilkinson, the first Black ballerina with the Ballet Russe de Monte Carlo, to take the stage in Atlanta, Georgia, in 1957, mere hours after being thrown out of the "whites-only" hotel where the company was staying and relegated to the "Colored" hotel on the other side of town. I felt in my bones the courage and emotional discipline that it took for Judge Brown Jackson to sit in that Senate chamber, the portrait of dignity. There was nothing to be gained by "going off." Part of the price of being the "first" is taking the body blows and keeping your eyes on the prize. Judge Ketanji Brown Jackson sat alone but stood for so many. She stood for everyone who had striven to break a barrier and reach the pinnacle in a country that for most of its history has relegated African Americans and other people of color to second-class citizenship.

Since the founding of our country, we African Americans have had to petition for the recognition of our full humanity, let alone equality. Like every Black ballet dancer I knew, I'd experienced the discounting of my abilities purely based on the refusal to see Black people as equals, capable of succeeding in traditionally "European" art forms. Throughout our careers, we were confronted with people who doubted that we "belonged" and saw us as unworthy of practicing the art form in which we'd trained for most of our lives.

From the time a serious practice of ballet was first brought to the United States by Russians fleeing the Revolution, Black dancers had aspired, like other Americans, to learn this classical dance form. Long before Arthur Mitchell founded the Dance Theatre of Harlem in 1969, in the wake of the assassination of Dr. Martin Luther King Jr., there were the American Negro Ballet and the New York Negro Ballet. When white conservatories wouldn't accept students of color in Washington, DC (a common form of discrimination in dance schools across the country), two courageous Black women, Doris W. Jones and Claire H. Haywood, founded the Jones-Haywood Dance School in 1941. Back then, and even at times still today, Black ballet dancers have been told it is not "our" art form, that our bodies and technique are not "refined" enough. Why were white people born in America, who hadn't danced ballet before it was introduced to this country in the late nineteenth and early twentieth centuries, any more qualified to dance it than Black people were? Ballet quickly became yet another wedge to divide the people of our country and the world into the "civilized" and the "uncivilized," the "true citizens" and the "outsiders."

Throughout my career, like so many other Black dancers, people have wanted to push me toward modern dance, which is considered freer, "wilder," and therefore more suitable to someone of my heritage. Yet my dream was ballet from my first class at thirteen, wearing gym shorts on a basketball court at the Boys and Girls Club of San Pedro. It was the dream of Erica Lall, Courtney Lavine, Aesha Ash, Tai Jimenez, Janet Collins, Céline Gittens, Marion Cuyjet, Delores Browne, Virginia Johnson, Alicia Graf Mack, Joan Myers Brown, Anne Benna Sims, and my mentor, Raven Wilkinson. Like Raven, several of the ballerinas I mentioned were first exposed to the art form when their parents took them to a performance of the Ballet Russe de Monte Carlo, the most famous touring company of the thirties, forties, and fifties.

People sometimes dismiss the performing arts as peripheral, a nonessential luxury, and yet our national identity is defined in part by our culture. To be marginalized from a culture is to be marginalized from citizenship. The pandemic, and more recently, the war in Ukraine have reminded us of the vital role the arts play in asserting our common humanity. Whether it's Tony Award winner Brian Stokes Mitchell singing from his balcony on the Upper West Side every night in the depths of sheltering in place during the pandemic or pianists playing for arriving Ukrainian refugees as they crossed the Polish border, such artistic expressions of empathy may not have saved lives, but they restored hope by reminding us of our capacity to create remarkable beauty in the midst of suffering.

As I finished watching the Supreme Court confirmation hearings, I was filled with a sense of sorrow. One senator had waxed nostalgic about the "good old days," when a white male nominee had been peacefully and uneventfully confirmed in a matter of hours…back in 1798. Then a right-wing pundit demanded that Judge Brown Jackson produce her LSAT scores to prove her worthiness. Clearly, in spite of the progress that her nomination is supposed to represent, the racial hierarchy and the coded language that reinforces it are still very much alive. Black Lives Matter becomes as much a question as a statement when we read the news and witness the continuing verbal and physical brutality against Black people.

On that March night, I felt the anxiety of every Black parent who wonders how to teach their child to reach for the sky, that anything is possible, when some still don't believe you deserve to even be "in the room." I felt the anxiety that all parents feel about the state of the world and the particular fear of Black mothers for the actual physical safety of their sons. Over the years, I've learned to look to lessons from the past to help answer questions about the future. So, in this moment I called upon the spirit of one of my guiding lights, Raven Wilkinson, the first Black woman to receive a contract with a major ballet company—in 1955, when full-on discrimination was actually legal in the United States.

Reflecting on Raven's remarkable journey and undefeatable faith and optimism reminded me that the source of power and dignity that Black Americans have cultivated over four hundred years is stronger than any racist theory: our tradition of the elders mentoring the young, both within families and with "chosen family." Because there are so many barriers left to break, we are completely dependent upon one another, and the person on whose shoulders we stand owns our "firsts" as much as we do. Whether in medicine, law, business, politics, or the arts, our elders' sacrifices and suffering were the down payment on our opportunities, and therefore our triumphs are their triumphs. What one generation begins, another finishes.

Opera singer Camilla Williams, the first Black woman to sing a lead role at the New York City Opera, paved the way for Marian Anderson's debut at the Metropolitan Opera twelve years later. Thanks to actress Diahann Carroll, who was the first Black woman to star in her own network series, Kerry Washington, Tracee Ellis Ross, Viola Davis, and dozens of others now routinely star in successful shows and films. Constance Baker Motley, the first Black female federal judge, forged a path for Judge Ketanji Brown Jackson, the first African American female Supreme Court justice. Alvin Ailey founded a groundbreaking interracial American dance company. At his request, former dancer Judith Jamison took over for him and made it one of the most successful dance organizations in the world. Anne Raven Wilkinson, who became the first Black ballerina in the Ballet Russe de Monte Carlo, among others, created a path for me. My journey would have been impossible without her career, her example, her love, and her friendship. I would never have become the first African American female principal dancer with American Ballet Theatre, America's national ballet company, without her. She passed away in the winter of 2018, but I carry her with me every day and in all that I do.

Raven taught me through her example that, as they say, "When and where I enter, the whole race enters with me" is not just a burden and a pressure, but it offers the promise of possibility. Once we break a barrier or shatter a glass ceiling, we make it possible for other dreamers to enter the space that once excluded us and thrive. Raven's teachings have given meaning to every plié I do and every performance I give. She showed me that we dance for all those who came before us and the many who will hopefully come after us. She held my hand through the ups and downs of my career. In her own life, she kept her head high through the "one step forward, two steps back" dance of civil rights in our country. And in spite of all she endured, she never surrendered to bitterness. Of all the gifts Raven gave me, one of the greatest was the gift of hope.

Some dreamers never get to meet their heroes and inspirations. How lucky I was to travel an important part of the road of life with mine. In Raven's spirit of love and generosity, I share our story.

Raven was and remains "the wind at my back." For all those dreaming an "impossible dream," I hope you find the wind at yours.

CHAPTER 1

IT ALL BEGAN TONIGHT

It's 6:47 p.m., and beads of sweat drip down my face before dropping to the studio floor. It has already been a long day of back-to-back rehearsals, which began at noon, preceded by daily ballet class. My muscles ache, my tired feet feel cemented in my pointe shoes, and my mind is racing with anticipation. It is the worst possible luck to have the last rehearsal of the day, scheduled from 6:00 p.m. to 7:00 p.m., when all I can think about is this evening's event. But right now, at this very minute, my focus must be on landing atop my partner's shoulder, arms crossed and chin high in the air, as if I hadn't a care in the world.

I finished rehearsing the pas de deux as the Milkmaid, a featured role in the ballet *The Bright Stream*, and quickly glanced up at the clock looming above the mirror on the far wall of

Studio 1 at 890 Broadway, American Ballet Theatre's rehearsal home in New York City. I had exactly forty-three minutes to shower, change, and make it uptown for a meeting I would later realize I'd waited my entire career for. Kevin McKenzie, our artistic director, and Alexei Ratmansky, the artist in residence choreographing the piece, huddled, speaking in hushed tones. We, the dancers, never knew if they were dissecting our performances or analyzing the steps of a particular sequence. Either way, the minutes ticked by as my eyes darted back up to the clock. I hoped my impatience wasn't too obvious. Disrespect for the process is not appreciated in a ballet company, especially one of ABT's international stature. Whether you are in the corps de ballet, a principal dancer, or like me at the time, in the middle, a soloist, you are meant to show gratitude for being part of this hallowed organization, not sit around grumbling and tapping your pointe shoes if they keep you in rehearsal until 7:00 p.m.

That attitude check is top of mind for the very few dancers of color. At that point in 2011, there were three of us in a company of eighty. I couldn't exactly say, "Hey, Kevin, Alexei, can we move this along? I've got someplace else to be." Especially then. Still striving to reach the rank of principal, it was as important as ever that I demonstrate my commitment to ABT and its process. And I always did...I just wished that I didn't need to demonstrate that enduring loyalty tonight.

I held my breath as Kevin and Alexei marked steps together. Were they going to ask me to start again? Was Alexei choosing this moment to make adjustments to the choreography? 6:50. I shook the tension out of my shoulders. This was the life I had chosen. It was not just a career; it was a calling. There's no crying or complaining in ballet...at least not in this current predicament. I had to focus. And at least my hair was done, swept up into a sleek ponytail. I could do my makeup in the cab.

After two more minutes that stretched on like hours, Alexei turned to us and said, "Thank you, dancers. We'll pick this up again tomorrow. Nice work." I was so relieved. My entire body relaxed. I nodded and smiled. Then, instinctually, I waited just one more beat to see if they had any specific notes to give me. Thankfully, Kevin and Alexei turned back to each other to continue their conversation. I ran to the side wall, grabbed my bag, and raced through the hallways to the shower, like Cinderella running out of the ball as the clock struck midnight. I got to the dressing room. 6:55. I had just enough time to shower and make it uptown. When you grow up in a family of six children, you learn to shower and dress in three minutes flat.

7:01. I was out on Broadway and Nineteenth Street, sweating and makeup-less, but showered and looking for a taxi. I saw a bright yellow light and hailed. Thanking God, I slid into the back seat. "144 West 125th Street, please," I said. My luck was turning. As we drove past the majestic Beaux-Arts buildings lining that stretch of downtown Broadway, I rolled down the window to breathe in the beautiful May evening breeze. This was always my favorite time of year in New York: the balmy weather, glorious sunsets at seven, and the anticipation of ABT's Metropolitan Opera House season. The season after which promotions were announced. It always felt like a time of possibility.

I pulled out my makeup bag to transform myself from rehearsal-disheveled "bunhead" to something approaching presentable. It was getting dark, so I turned on the light. My tiny compact mirror wasn't ideal, but after so many years of being on the road, I could apply makeup in the dark.

In a New York minute my luck turned upside down, when I looked away from my compact to see the traffic conspiring against me. Madison Avenue was a disaster. We slowed to a crawl. The lights changed, but we barely moved. It was 7:15, and we were only at Forty-Second Street. How would I ever make it to 125th Street by 7:30? And I'd wanted to arrive early. Should I jump out and head toward the subway? I wondered. No, the station was too far east. I'd have to run, the train would be jam-packed at this hour, and I'd have to let two pass before finding one I could get on.

7:19. Nothing to do but sit back and pray. Even if I was late, the evening was still happening. We caught a break after Sixty-Fifth Street. Traffic cleared. "Could you go just a little bit faster?" I urged the driver. And he obliged, speeding up the avenue. Miraculously, within eight minutes, we arrived at 144 West 125th Street, the five-story home of the Studio Museum in Harlem. I paid the fare and jumped out of the cab.

I pushed the glass doors open and entered the foyer. To my

left, I saw a crowd of one hundred or so people sitting in the museum's atrium auditorium, waiting for the program to begin. In the back I spotted my friend Alek Wek, a South Sudanese supermodel, and Olu, my then ex-boyfriend. He smiled in his warm way and waved. He knew how much this evening meant, and he'd taken the time to come even though we were no longer together. That meant a lot. I turned around to see my manager, Gilda Squire, and a member of the museum staff who welcomed me. Gilda grabbed my dance bag as they rushed me to a side room, and there she stood: five foot two but with the spirit of a giant, the woman I'd unknowingly been searching for my entire life, the woman who'd made my way in classical ballet possible, Raven Wilkinson.

Tears immediately filled my eyes. I was overcome with emotion. As soon as I saw Raven, everyone else's face and voice faded away, and I could only focus on her. Raven beamed as I approached her, her smile as bright and warm as the sun. She hugged me. Her embrace felt like coming home. She grasped my hands and said, "I've waited so long to meet you. I've followed your story since you were fifteen and won the Music Center Spotlight competition. You are exquisite." That was one of the greatest accolades of my life. To hear that a woman who'd blazed the trail for me, a woman I revered, had been watching *my* career since the beginning made me feel seen and affirmed as nothing else ever had. It was like receiving a blessing. I couldn't believe it. I had to repeat what she said in my head. Raven

Wilkinson, a pioneer, had been watching *me*. I *had* found my fairy godmother.

We could have stood there all night expressing our mutual adoration, but Gilda politely yet firmly said, "Ladies, we can continue this later. The panel discussion needs to begin." Walking arm in arm, Raven and I stepped out onto the little platform to begin our first "performance" as a duo, and the friendship that would become my North Star.

CHAPTER 2

A DISTANT MIRROR

The first time I encountered Raven, a year earlier, in the spring of 2010, was much less eventful than that incredible night at the Studio Museum in Harlem.

I was unwinding from an eight-hour rehearsal day in my Upper West Side apartment. Sipping a glass of prosecco and finally taking a moment to exhale, I decided to watch a DVD of a dance documentary given out to company members at ABT titled *Ballets Russes*. It tells the story of the two famous ballet companies that were among the first to bring the European art form of ballet to the United States. But for me, this documentary gave me so much more. I was introduced for a few brief moments to the story and legacy of a woman who nearly sixty years earlier was on the same path I was currently on as a Black ballerina:

Raven Wilkinson. Little did I know that a quiet evening at home watching a ballet documentary would quite literally change my entire outlook on my life and career.

At this point I had been a soloist with ABT for three years. This meant that I had been promoted from the corps de ballet, the group of sixty hardworking dancers who framed the solo artists and created the atmosphere onstage. With this promotion came dreams of what more the future might hold for me, but in truth, these hopes seemed nothing more than fantasy when faced with the sobering history of the lack of diversity in ballet and ABT specifically. Having joined ABT's Studio Company in 2000 and ABT's main company in 2001, I was the only Black woman in the company for the first ten years of my career. And there hadn't been another Black female at ABT for decades before me. For me, the bleakness of looking forward made looking backward that much more necessary. I was searching for inspiration in a history that I hoped existed but I had not yet found.

After six years of dancing the role of one of the peasant girls celebrating the harvest in *Giselle*, as a townsperson of Verona in *Romeo and Juliet*, and one in a really, really long line of swan maidens in *Swan Lake*, I now danced only featured roles. Just one other African American woman had ever reached that level with the company, Anne Benna Sims in the 1970s. And, ironically, I hadn't learned about her until *after* I was promoted. It seemed as if the stories of other Black ballerinas, including Ms.

Sims, had been erased or forgotten. I never heard anyone speak about her. As the second Black woman soloist in ABT's seventy-one-year history, I wanted to live up to that responsibility and honor.

As a dancer you're forever a student, and as the saying goes, only as good as your last performance—and that meant constant preparation, onstage and off. So, during my subway rides to and from company class and rehearsal, I'd listen to the music of the ballets I was rehearsing. And on many nights, I watched videos to see some of the world's best dancers, past and present, dance iconic roles I hoped to perform one day. Natalia Makarova as Nikiya in *La Bayadère*. Alessandra Ferri as Juliet in *Romeo and Juliet*. Paloma Herrera as Kitri in *Don Quixote*. Nina Ananiashvili as Odette/Odile in *Swan Lake*. All of them were spectacular dancers. All of them were white.

Was it naive to even dream of being the ballet equivalent of the "leading lady," an honored place that had rarely been granted to Black women on the big or small screen, or in the theater? The odds were even more daunting in classical ballet. For now I couldn't allow myself to focus on the answer to that question. I was just going to continue to work, even if the goal still seemed out of reach. Regardless, I was as committed and determined as ever to learn everything I could about the history of this art form that I loved and had given my life to.

That night's history lesson, the aforementioned documentary *Ballets Russes*, featured Freddie Franklin, an elegant

Englishman and premier danseur with the Ballet Russe de Monte Carlo who now worked with ABT, staging ballets by choreographers Léonide Massine, Michel Fokine, and more, some of which were originally created for him. On-screen, he had the same warmth and humor that I knew from our interactions in the studio and backstage at the Metropolitan Opera House.

The documentary was full of other ballet giants, like George Balanchine, who went on to found the New York City Ballet (NYCB). The film covered him when he was an up-and-coming choreographer from Russia. The beautiful Native American prima ballerina Maria Tallchief, who became a founding member of the New York City Ballet and one of Balanchine's wives and muses, was shown describing Balanchine's bizarre and unexpected marriage proposal. He was choreographing pieces for the Ballet Russe and retraining Maria in his own pared-down version of the classic dance form. One day he said, "We must marry." She replied, "I don't love you." He countered, "Don't worry. Love will come." And so, they wed on August 16, 1946, when she was nineteen. Several months later, she left with him when he formed his company, then called Ballet Society, which, as Freddie Franklin put it in the film, was centered on ballets with "no scenery, no costumes, and lots of lovely music." There were also several Russian former prima ballerinas in the documentary, wearing full onstage makeup and big chandelier earrings, ever the ballet divas. It all felt very familiar to me in terms of the ballet traditions I knew and the characters I'd met over the years.

Despite the presence of these ballet luminaries, it was a deep, soothing voice that filled my living room an hour and thirty-five minutes into the two-hour film that unexpectedly pulled my attention to the screen. There was a black-and-white image of what seemed to be a young ballerina of color auditioning for four white men in front of the mirror of a dance studio. "I had auditioned," the magnetic voice began, and then a beautiful older woman with café au lait skin and delicate features framed by wavy salt-and-pepper hair swept into a soft updo appeared on-screen. The chyron read "Raven Wilkinson." My heart stopped. I listened intently as this beautiful lady finished her sentence: "...two or three times and I wasn't ever chosen."

She held her head high, and her tone was calm as she explained how other dancers had told her she'd never be accepted into the prestigious Ballet Russe because of the color of her skin. I immediately sat up. Was I seeing what I thought I was seeing? A Black ballerina. Talking about her experiences with one of the most important dance companies of the twentieth century. A Black ballerina who had danced all over the United States of America, with a white company, in the 1950s, *the* height of segregation. And here she was telling her story—our story.

The film moved on to other dancers. I looked at my clock. There were twenty minutes left in the movie. I waited, hoping Raven Wilkinson would reappear on-screen. A few minutes later, she did. There were beautiful photographs of her in the principal role of a ballet I knew well, *Les Sylphides*. I couldn't believe it. There are so few Black women in ballet, let alone performing as one of the leads in a soft, romantic, and ethereal ballet like *Les Sylphides*. But there she was, the perfect sylph. Another two minutes and she was gone, only to reappear for a moment in one of the last scenes of the film, a reunion of all the dancers from the Ballet Russe, a member of the company, yet different. Just like me.

There was one photograph I couldn't get out of my head: a picture of the entire company, with Raven at the center, her big dark eyes staring straight ahead. Was she sad? Hopeful in spite of all the obstacles she faced? Proud? Like me, looking for acceptance? Or was she saying, "I belong"? In those few moments, I recognized and saw myself. I understood how Raven could have felt isolated as "the only," similar to my experience at ABT, until other dancers of color like Calvin Royal III and Courtney Lavine finally joined the corps de ballet. I knew this was a very lonely place to be. Seeing Raven on my television screen was like looking into a mirror. This woman had lived my experience, and frustratingly, not much had changed since 1955. But the documentary was only a small part of her story. I knew there was so much more to learn about Raven.

A fire was lit in me. How and why had I never heard of her before? Of course, I had read about Janet Collins, the first Black prima ballerina with the Metropolitan Opera. I had followed amazing groundbreaking dancers like Dance Theatre of Harlem's Virginia Johnson and Stephanie Dabney, and Houston Ballet's Lauren Anderson. But why hadn't I ever heard anyone talk about this pioneer? Why were Black women just "disappeared" and erased from ballet history? Why had she been slipped into the end of this film like an interesting footnote? Was she still alive? And if so, what was she doing? I felt compelled to know and learn everything about her.

I turned to the only tool I had: Google. Heartbreakingly, this pioneering ballerina didn't have a Wikipedia page. However, I did find interviews she'd given. I read them all and watched the ones available on YouTube. A few nights later, at the Metropolitan Opera House, I saw Freddie Franklin, her former colleague, backstage. I cornered him, asking him every question I could think of about her. What was she like? Had he ever partnered her? How did she survive the terrible things that happened when they traveled to the South? What was it like seeing her in *Les Sylphides*? Freddie's eyes lit up as he spoke about her.

"Raven!" he exclaimed, clapping his hands together. "She was quite simply one of the loveliest dancers I'd ever seen. I told Mr. Denham (the director of the Ballet Russe) we just had to hire her. And her feet!" In ballet, having perfectly arched feet is like having perfect pitch in singing.

"She was such a gentle soul," Freddie continued. "But what happened in the South. Well, it was just awful." I longed to hear more, but we were summoned to rehearsal. My brief exchange with Freddie only increased my passion to know more about my new idol.

Learning of Raven had given me a second wind and a purpose I had never felt before. Raven became more than a role model to me. She was an icon who made my dreams seem less impossible, who proved that my journey was not unprecedented, even though no one at ABT other than Freddie Franklin seemed to know anything about her. She was a hero who fought battles the rest of us can only imagine. I continued to look for any scrap of information I could find about her and shared her story whenever and wherever possible.

Because of the rarity of a Black woman holding the position of soloist at ABT, I was often invited to do interviews on television and in magazines about my career and experiences. And it was one of those appearances in early 2011 that led me to connecting with Raven at last. Gilda heard me speak about her during an interview for *BET Nightly News*. I told Ed Gordon, the host, that even though I'd never met Raven, her journey inspired me. I'd briefly shared her history, her experiences in the Jim Crow South, and how she'd eventually had to leave the United States to pursue her ballet career. Unbeknownst to me, this was the moment that Gilda decided to try to bring us together.

Finding Raven was no small feat because though Raven lived fully in the present, she didn't own a cell phone or a computer or go anywhere near the Internet. Like a great detective,

Gilda searched the Web and discovered that in the past couple of years, Raven had appeared on a panel alongside Dance Theatre of Harlem founder, Arthur Mitchell, at New York City Center. Gilda started by contacting City Center's public relations office, where she was told that Raven was reachable only through her home phone. The PR person agreed to pass Gilda's cell phone number along to Raven, but with no promise that we'd get a response.

A few days later, Gilda's phone rang, and it was Raven. As Gilda began to tell Raven about me, she politely stopped her midsentence. Raven shared that she'd followed my story since I first appeared on the classical ballet scene in my teen years and that she had attended almost all my performances with ABT in New York City. And ironically, Raven lived only blocks away from my apartment. All this time, Raven and I had admired each other from afar, only to learn that we lived in the same neighborhood but had never met. It was too wonderful to be true.

Raven was so warm and engaged that Gilda went out on a limb and asked if she'd be interested in joining me in a conversation centered around two generations of Black ballerinas at the Studio Museum in Harlem. Raven responded, "Tell me when and I'll be there."

When Gilda called to tell me that I would meet the woman who had quite literally blazed a trail for me, I cried, full of joy and gratitude. Just as I was beginning to lose faith in my future, my prayers were answered beyond my wildest dreams. I had found someone who connected me to a lineage in ballet, and she gave me a true sense of belonging. I would soon stand face-to-face with the woman who would show me that my career was about much more than just me.

CHAPTER 3

TWO WOMEN AT THE CROSSROADS

May 12, 2011. 8:10 p.m. The audience at the Studio Museum in Harlem hung on Raven's every word as she spoke of the thrill of dancing one of her favorite parts: the waltz solo in *Les Sylphides*, an abstract romantic ballet choreographed by Michel Fokine. Her face glowed as she described the feeling of leaping through the air dressed as an ethereal sylph. It was as if, even after all these years later, she could still hear Chopin's music in her head. It's true that once you dance a part you love, the melody never leaves you. It's in your bones. Raven exuded this love and so much more: strength, beauty, survival against impossible odds. I sat listening to her, mesmerized. It felt like a dream. I was speaking on a panel with a woman who had experienced so many of the highs and lows of my own journey: from feeling that I had to work harder than my colleagues to "earn my place" in an art form that traditionalists say "wasn't meant for you," to the exhilaration of losing yourself in a role. From the time I first saw her in the *Ballets Russes* documentary, Raven had given me a renewed sense of hope and belonging. And here I was, sitting beside her.

When Raven finished speaking, our moderator, Brenda Dixon Gottschild, an author, cultural historian, and dancer herself, opened the floor to audience questions. Most of the audience members were as amazed by Raven as I was. The crowd, young and old alike, started by thanking her for just *being*. She smiled her warm smile, nodded, and bowed her head. For a woman who lived a fairly private life once she left the stage, the public praise was overwhelming and something she visibly did not take for granted. She was humble and gracious.

The first question came from an elegant West Indian woman who wondered why there was such a pressure to conform to a super-lean body type when ballerinas had been full-figured in the nineteenth century.

"It was (acceptable) at that time, but that's definitely changed. It's no longer accepted," I responded. Then Raven added her special touch, saying, "That was a beautiful woman in those days. Now she's slightly overweight." The audience laughed. I did, too. This was my first small glimpse of Raven's irreverent humor. A young man stood up to state:

"George Balanchine made it very clear that with the women of the corps de ballet, he wanted their skin to be the color of the inside of a crisp apple. The ideal of a woman as a swan is white, so that's the benchmark that you're constantly fighting...New York City Ballet don't look like New York City. Everybody says that with male dancers of color, it's a little easier. I beg to differ, because I've spoken to Black male New York City Ballet dancers and they were stuck in the corps. They kept hitting ceilings. And they only got certain parts. The only person I know of to hold the rank of principal dancer in City Ballet after Arthur Mitchell is Albert Evans. And I know that Aesha Ash ran into the same problems."

"Is Louis Johnson in the audience?" Raven asked, referencing the legendary Black dancer and choreographer who had been a guest dancer with NYCB in the 1950s. Several people, including the moderator, answered, "Yes!" Many applauded, including Raven, one trailblazer saluting another.

"Now, that's somebody," Raven declared. "He should tell you his story, but I don't know if he will." Knowing Mr. Johnson was too self-effacing to take the stage, Raven continued: "Jerome Robbins worked with him in the *Afternoon of a Faun*. He did it for Jerome Robbins, fantastic choreographer. Ballet, opera, Broadway. I remember seeing him; he just bounded all over and pirouetted, all over the place zing, zing, zing."

This was my introduction to Raven's joyful, humorous, and highly visual way of describing movement. She continued on a slightly more somber note, "And yet he was denied the opportunity to have a fuller classical ballet career." We all absorbed the pain of that denial in spite of extraordinary talent. With this story, Raven reminded us of the common fate of so many Black dance prodigies, male or female, light skinned or dark complexioned. And with her trademark generosity, she reminded one of her contemporaries that she had witnessed his genius and his exclusion. Her brief remarks further opened my eyes to the magnificent community that had preceded me in my quest to join the ballet pantheon.

Yet another guest stood up to challenge us on our attachment to an art form that clearly didn't welcome us, saying:

"It seems like the story with a lot of Black folks when they hit a ceiling in other art forms is that they decide to go create their own work... You guys have decided to be in a certain type of dance and dance company where you say you have to work twice as hard as other people. I wonder why you make a decision to dance a type of dance, in a certain type of company, when you might have an opportunity to be in your own company and be in a more multicultural environment."

"It will never change if there isn't someone that stays and tries to make it happen," I replied. Raven quickly came to my defense:

"She told you how much it meant for her to join American Ballet Theatre and to be a part of this. And this is something to be celebrated because that dream is being accomplished now.

And if we just go off and always do our own thing, it's an ensemble effort, life, our culture is. And so, it has to be in all its areas, and we have to endeavor to make it that way. By just doing what we do, by quietly being there, doing the best that we can do, like Misty's doing."

I continued. "I do ballet because it's what I love to do and it's what I love. There are so many Black dancers who get discouraged and are told to be modern dancers. This cycle has to stop." Expanding on my point, Raven shared a story that resonated with me and every Black ballet dancer in the audience, the constant challenging of our suitability to dance ballet, a European art form. In her case, absurdly, one such challenge occurred when she was auditioning for the Joffrey Ballet company's production of a new piece about the civil rights movement titled *These Three*, choreographed by Eugene Loring. Raven began, "Mr. Joffrey asked me to come and audition. After class, he (Loring) said, 'Your ballet's fine. Now let me see your modern.' I said, 'I really don't know modern.' We really didn't study it in those days. So, he requested I do some classic modern dance moves. And I was trying so hard, but I could tell that he was getting frustrated with my inability to execute the moves like a modern dancer." Raven continued. "Finally, I said, 'Mr. Loring, I've been a ballet dancer all my life. I know it's hard for you to imagine. But here I am. I was in the Ballet Russe. I'm not a modern dancer.'" In that moment, I found myself nodding vigorously in agreement with this sentiment. She was expressing

31

the longing and frustration many Black classical ballet dancers feel: to be seen and accepted as simply the classical ballet dancers we've trained to be.

Finally, a man stood up and stated that he knew many young Black girls who were brown and dark complexioned who had seen the more fair-skinned girls have an opportunity in ballet while their hopes were dashed. I'd been asked on several occasions about the role my complexion has played in my career. It's a fair question. We can't ignore the fact that there are varying forms of privilege both in the world and in ballet. So, I understand why people ask. As in so many other fields in America, there is an arbitrary system set up to decide what kind of "Blackness" is "acceptable."

Colorism is very real within the Black community and beyond, and it certainly has played a role in both Raven's and my access and opportunity within ballet. But, of course, that does not exclude lighter-skinned Black people from discrimination or being considered "other." Black dancers are not a monolith, and my feeling and hope are that the success of any of us can help open the door, even if only incrementally wider, for the success of us all. This belief only made me work harder to make a space for more dancers of color. We all deserved to be represented. But that night, I struggled for the right words with which to respond. Raven leaned into her microphone. Many in the audience nodded in agreement as she succinctly and easily made clear that we were *all* struggling against a system that hadn't been created for us and that for most of history, hadn't even acknowledged our existence. She said:

"We have enough respect for the ballet and love for it to hope that it opens up. Because culturally, we're all in it together in this country, and we have to learn to share each other's cultures and be a part of it. That's the constant... journey. But if you love ballet and you respect it, you want to see it open up to its fullness. Because that's how it's going to last... It can't be on a dusty shelf back in the 1800s."

A few moments later, Brenda announced it was time to end the program. As she thanked us for our participation, the audience erupted into applause.[1] This would be the first time that Raven and I took a bow together.

Gilda guided Raven and me to the reception room, where waiters served drinks and hors d'oeuvres, and the crowd began to gather. The Studio Museum always drew a large, eclectic audience of young professionals, older neighborhood intellectuals, and artists. I didn't want to leave Raven's side. And I wasn't alone. So many attendees wanted to speak with her, and she made each person who approached her feel welcome. My friends who'd come to support me made their way to us one by one.

Raven wanted to meet everyone. There was Alek Wek, who had escaped the war in South Sudan and become a supermodel in the nineties, setting a new standard for beauty. Having been the first African model to appear on the cover of *ELLE* magazine, Alek certainly understood what it meant to be an "only" or "other" in the fashion world, which has faced its own denunciations of the lack of diversity and inclusion for Black models. Alek hugged me and gushed over Raven.

An entire group from Dance Theatre of Harlem came to pay their respects to Raven, a woman who had also helped make their careers possible. Raven was especially curious about the young man with a sparkle in his eyes and the bright smile who lingered at the back of the room. Raven locked eyes with Olu and was instantly smitten. Olu approached. He'd come all the way from his office in Midtown to share this special night with me. And I admit, I was touched and more than a bit excited. Raven could sense the connection between us that was still there. She had a way about her in social settings. It didn't really matter who her audience was; she would turn on the charm. She flirted with Olu and made cheeky remarks that made him blush. "Well, aren't you easy on the eyes?" she said as I introduced them. He was always so self-possessed, but Raven's playful teasing threw him.

As he walked away, Raven turned to me and asked, "And who was that lovely drink of water? There's many a woman who'd let him put his shoes under her bed..."

I laughed. Raven was so refined and elegant and then so effortlessly spicy. It was unexpected and completely delightful.

"Well," she pressed, "I know there's a story there. I could see the way he looked at you. And the way you didn't mind being looked at."

I explained we'd broken up about seven months before but remained good friends. She couldn't understand why we were no longer a couple. "It's not my business, and I don't know the details. I'll just say that any young man who'd come all this way to see you talk to an old lady must really care. That's a phone number I wouldn't lose if I were in your shoes," she insisted. I took her words in. We'd only just met, but already I knew Raven had stores of wisdom to impart. Most of the time, she shared her advice indirectly, through stories. But she was crystal clear about Olu right from the start.

This was a big evening for me in so many ways. I realized as I stood in that room that I was surrounded by a newer group of people whom I had grown close to, personally and professionally, since Olu and I had broken up. Olu had been such a big part of my life for seven years, from the time I was twenty-one years old, and through him, I'd learned so much about myself as a woman and as a dancer beyond the stage. He had been more than my partner; he was my friend and chief adviser. And though he remained present in my life, he was no longer in my everyday circle.

In the time we'd been apart, I'd built a team to lean on for advice, support, and counsel as I looked to progress in my career. Gilda became my manager, and I began taking on a lot of newer responsibilities, including speaking to children in schools about the benefits of the arts. This was a huge step for me because I was not at all comfortable speaking in front of crowds. I was severely introverted as a child and was even nicknamed "Mouse" because I was so quiet. Silence had always been my armor and my refuge in the chaos of my upbringing. I was the fourth of six children born to a beautiful, dynamic mother with a habit of marrying the "wrong" men. Growing up, we never knew what the next day, month, or year would bring. The only constant was uncertainty, both emotional and economic. We might find ourselves living comfortably in a large house by the water in San Pedro one day and packing up all our belongings in a car and driving hundreds of miles the next. We moved constantly, and even for a time lived in one room of a motel. Like many children navigating such instability, I retreated into my own cocoon of imagination and observed the people and the world around me, ever on the alert for the next upheaval. It wasn't until I discovered ballet that I found a true sanctuary and my "voice." I was always much more at ease dancing on the stage; that was my form of communicating with an audience. But Gilda pushed me to go outside my comfort zone to share my journey and potentially inspire others.

I was also growing as an artist and pursuing opportunities to perform beyond the studios of ABT. I'd been personally invited by the iconic musician Prince to join his Welcome 2 America tour, and I had spent a lot of my downtime from ABT working with Dance Theatre of Harlem in the studio as they created new works for the company's return to the stage after an eight-year hiatus.

I was experiencing so many fulfilling artistic adventures and had almost begun to fly, which I never thought I'd be able to do without Olu. He was my first boyfriend and had helped me find my voice and confidence at ABT in a crucial period in my career; I depended on him. His encouragement and perspective were vital to my growth as a young woman. But now I was surrounded by, and leaning on, an incredible group of strong Black women, Raven among them. This sisterhood supported me as I learned to stand on my own, something that was important for me to do before I could truly be in a committed relationship. The women I'd invited crowded around me, all wanting to know, "Was that *him*? *The* Olu." They all seemed to have an extra pep in their step knowing that he was back on the market. Raven's words rang in my ears. She was right. That night represented a beautiful effort on Olu's part. Though we'd needed the time apart to grow as individuals, his coming that night showed how much he still cared about me as a person and that he knew how much Raven meant to me.

The entire night felt like a dream, but the best part was speaking with Raven, just the two of us. She immediately dove in with me like we were old friends. She wanted to know if I was happy and how things really were for me at ABT. I was comfortable with her right away and was easily candid with her from the start.

I explained that ABT's spring season at the Metropolitan Opera House opened in less than a week. I had been a soloist for four years and was gearing up for the most important season of our year, which was a big point of stress, excitement, and possibility. This was the time of year when the artistic director of the company zoned in and focused on how each dancer was progressing and promotions typically happened at the end of the season. So, despite all the excitement and buildup around this evening and getting to meet Raven, the spring season was still looming over me.

I confided in Raven that I felt like my career was in limbo and that it was learning about her that had given me the second wind I needed to keep pushing. She shook her head, like she was shaking off the praise. She could never accept these types of compliments. In her humble way, she said what became a refrain, "You had that in you already." There is no bigger gift than someone you admire believing in you when you don't fully believe in yourself.

She asked me what role I was most excited to dance that spring, and again, being completely honest with her, I said there weren't any roles that I was terribly excited about. After eleven years with ABT, there were no new or interesting parts that gave me hope I would ever rise beyond the rank of soloist. I explained that I did enjoy finding new ways to challenge myself within the roles I had danced many times, like a flower girl in *Don Quixote* or the peasant pas de deux in *Giselle*. I was constantly striving to meet my own expectations of excellence. I enjoy being able to take on the characters I'm portraying, and in that moment, bring who I am to them. A ballerina's version of "There are no small parts, only small actors." But it was often deflating not knowing if there was a plan or trajectory for me within the company.

Raven could completely relate to this way of approaching performing. Finding ways of challenging yourself and not only performing for the audience but for your fulfillment as well. Embracing the characters and using them to fuel your performance. She told me how alive and present she felt onstage and how her goal always was to *be* the character, not just to play it. Raven told me that night that she planned to attend every one of my upcoming performances that spring season. She said she was especially looking forward to seeing me as the Milkmaid in Alexei Ratmansky's *The Bright Stream*. Then she said the words that would become her mantra and my lifeline: "Every time you step on that stage, I'll be the wind at your back." I was overcome with emotion. I couldn't believe how connected we were so quickly. I truly believed that she would be the wind at my back that I'd been searching for my whole career, that extra push to help me prove not only to the world, but also to myself, that I'm enough.

We stayed at the museum chatting until finally a staff member came and politely reminded us that they needed to close. I could have stayed there all night talking to her, but I had to get home and to bed to face a full day of rehearsals the next day. I needed to have all my energy to perfect my Milkmaid and Flower Girl. After all, in a few weeks, I'd be performing these roles for an audience of four thousand...and Raven.

That night, I think we both felt we had been brought together for a reason. I had been stuck, not progressing to the next level, and was beginning to lose hope that I ever would. This wasn't an uncommon experience among dancers in the company, but American Ballet Theatre had *never* had a Black female principal dancer. At the same time, at the age of seventy-six, the curtain had just closed on Raven's performing career at the New York City Opera. She'd worked there for thirty years, first as a dancer and then as a character actress, but the Opera had recently lost its home at Lincoln Center. Raven was a woman born to be on a stage, and now she was figuring out her "next act," her purpose. Some friendships renew your hope and faith, and you are reborn. That night changed both our lives. And for the first time in my career, I knew I was no longer alone. I had the wind at my back.

Haute Harlem

From the time I first met her, Raven spoke often and lovingly about her family. Something I really enjoyed listening to, as I would come to learn just how private Raven was about many other aspects of her life, a trait I feel was common for her generation. When she was born, in 1935, Franklin Delano Roosevelt was president, the country was in the midst of the Great Depression, the Harlem Renaissance was in full swing, and American Ballet Theatre had yet to be founded. In this time of pain and possibility, the Wilkinson home was an oasis of calm, love, and achievement. Quite a contrast to my own chaotic household growing up with five siblings and a single mom. Raven's father, Frost Birnie Wilkinson, who had matriculated through Dartmouth College in three years as a member of the class of 1928 and gone on to Harvard's School of Dentistry, ran a successful practice in Harlem. Her mother, Anne James Wilkinson, was a homemaker. They lived with their two children, son

Frost Wilkinson II and daughter Anne Raven, in the elegant Paul Laurence Dunbar Garden Apartments, built by John D. Rockefeller as the first co-op apartments created specifically for African Americans. Over the years, its notable residents included W. E. B. Du Bois, Paul Robeson, Bill "Bojangles" Robinson, and polar explorer Matthew Henson.[2] In later years, the family moved to a gracious prewar building on Riverside Drive, with sweeping views of the Hudson.

As children, Raven and her brother attended the progressive private Ethical Culture School. Her family took full advantage of the city's rich artistic life, frequently going to museums, the theater, and the symphony. But one cultural outing in Raven's young life stood out among all others: her first time at the ballet. And she loved telling the story. She was five years old, and her parents brought her to a matinee of the famed Ballet Russe de Monte Carlo. This touring company featured some of the greatest international dancers of the day and introduced audiences across America, Black and white, to the ballet art form. The performance that day was of Marius Petipa's *Coppélia*, with the great Alexandra Danilova and Freddie Franklin dancing the leads. Based on a fantastical short story by E. T. A. Hoffmann, it tells the tale of Dr. Coppelius who has made a dancing doll so lifelike that it inspires a village boy, Franz, to abandon his beloved, Swanilda, who in turn impersonates the doll to win Franz back.

Even in her seventies, Raven could remember the powerful

emotion that swept over her as she sat in her red velvet seat in the enormous City Center auditorium, listening to the overture. The music literally moved her to tears, and then, for the next two hours, she sat transfixed, watching the dancers bring this fairy tale to magical life. Between Raven's reaction to this performance and her constant dancing around their apartment, Anne Wilkinson knew she had to find classes for her daughter. As Raven herself explained, "From the time I was a little girl and was able to walk, I would dance. I guess I just always loved dance. I suppose my mother felt after a while she should give me some guidance in it."[3] Anne Wilkinson began by trying to enroll her daughter at New York City Ballet's conservatory, the School of American Ballet, then in its infancy. They told her Raven was too young and recommended the Dalcroze method, a combination of eurhythmics and dance, where musicality is developed through rhythmic movement.

After four years of this instruction, Raven's destiny was set when her uncle gave her ballet classes as a birthday present. In February 1944, nine-year-old Raven arrived at Madame Maria Swoboda's dance school on West Fifty-Seventh Street. Madame Swoboda and her husband, Vecheslav, had been lead dancers at the Bolshoi Theatre in Moscow. They left in 1917 during the Revolution and, like so many other Russian dancers, came to the United States as stars in the 1930s. Like me, Raven took her first ballet class in gym shorts. But that is where the resemblance between our childhoods ends.

Raven described not loving the classes at first; they were such a departure from the freedom of the eurythmics at Dalcroze. "It took me forever to learn the difference between an échappé and an assemblé and I found it all very boring. And I thought 'what did I get myself into? This isn't dancing,' but I soon got over that...I would die to dance."[4] She was bitten by the bug and fascinated by the regal and demanding Madame Swoboda. "She was like some princess to me," she would say.

Raven's devoted parents wanted to give her an excellent education. Like many children with a great artistic gift, she faced a fork in the road. Her ballet classes four times a week interfered with the demands of her school schedule. And the reality of race was in the back of their minds, which, as Raven often said, they didn't speak of overtly. "My parents didn't put that before me... They wanted me to develop...my confidence as a human being, but yet, it was a reality."[5]

Raven's mother went to Madame Swoboda to ask her honest opinion of Raven's future potential as a dancer. The Wilkinsons wanted to know if this was a realistic path for their daughter. Madame Swoboda assured them that Raven was one of her finest students. Raven's parents transferred her to the Professional Children's School so that she'd have the flexibility to get the ballet training she needed to pursue a real career. In keeping with her family's belief in higher education, she enrolled as a student at Columbia University after high school, and she kept a busy schedule of traveling uptown for classes and to Midtown to dance.

But the biggest tests lay ahead, when she auditioned for the company that had first ignited her passion for the art form to which she hoped to devote her life. As she often told me, "I wanted more than anything to become a ballet dancer."

This feeling is as old and common among us as is the ballet technique itself, and most dancers feel this way. Ballet is what we need to do to even breathe. But hearing it from a woman who faced the same obstacles as me, and more, affirmed me in my path. Raven's family also served as such an example of triumphing against the times and the odds in a world that ignores your existence or erases you altogether. The Wilkinsons represented a world of possibility and achievement that we don't learn about in school and don't often see represented in media. It was inspiring to learn about them through Raven's vivid memories. It was almost as much of a revelation as seeing her in the documentary for the first time.

CHAPTER 4

NEVER GIVE UP

The least I could do was try.

—RAVEN WILKINSON

Mid-June is one of my favorite times of the year, with warm evening breezes, Central Park in full emerald bloom, and we're almost halfway through the exhilarating but grueling Met season. The year I met Raven, that season was even sweeter, filled with milestones that were the talk of the dance world. Principal dancer José Manuel Carreño danced his final New York performance with ABT after sixteen years, dancing as Prince Siegfried in *Swan Lake* opposite principal dancer Julie Kent as Odette and Gillian Murphy as Odile, while Julie also celebrated her twenty-fifth anniversary with the company, dancing John Neumeier's *Lady of the Camellias* on her special night. Another principal dancer, Hee Seo, made her debut as the lead in *Giselle*, one of ABT's signature story ballets. And the company's resident choreographer, Alexei Ratmansky, premiered *The Bright Stream*, with principal dancers Paloma Herrera, Marcelo Gomes, Gillian Murphy, and David Hallberg in the lead roles.

As a soloist, I danced in much of the spring season repertoire while also continuing to work toward having an opportunity to take on a lead role. Still, it was a fulfilling Met season, and I was looking forward to finishing up as we always did on the July Fourth weekend, then heading to Los Angeles for our annual summer season there. Just as she promised, Raven attended every single one of my performances in New York. We were developing a beautiful friendship and routine. I'd see her after performances, and we'd often walk out the stage door and into the night together, slowly strolling home. We'd meet for dinner on weekends at Café Luxembourg, a lively French brasserie in our Upper West Side neighborhood. And we spent hours on the phone at least once a week.

Our conversations were always full of love and depth. They covered the gamut from dance to my personal life. What made Raven a unique mentor was the way in which she approached giving me advice and feedback. As a former dancer and my elder, you would think she'd have given me specific corrections or ways to improve my dancing, but it was always deeper than that with her. I had coaches and teachers who fulfilled that need; Raven supported and encouraged me not just as a ballerina but as a woman who was beginning to see a purpose beyond my performances.

We'd begin by talking about my approach to a character or the physical challenges of a variation, and then Raven would gently probe what I was feeling, often by sharing an anecdote from her past. For me, growing up in a large family with a mother who was just trying to ensure we had a roof over our heads and enough to eat, I learned to keep my emotions to myself. Raven's gentle manner and infinite patience helped me to open up about my deepest fears, that like so many other Black ballerinas before me, I wouldn't get to see the full realization of my dream: that one day I could shatter the glass ceiling.

Raven never lectured. She just shared her truths. She began to speak with me about how she'd auditioned several times for the Ballet Russe, and despite not being chosen, she never gave up. She talked to me about her experiences traveling with Ballet Russe in the Jim Crow South in the 1950s and early 1960s, when she was singled out for being Black and her life was threatened merely because she was a Black ballerina on tour with the company. She also told me about her decision to leave behind everything she knew in America to head to Amsterdam to dance with the Dutch National Ballet just so she could continue her career, something she did not feel would be possible in the United States.

Of course, not every conversation was about the challenges and obstacles she faced. She also brought what I came to know as her unique Raven "light" to our talks, sharing stories about her career that would have me in stitches. Despite her elegance and sophistication, Raven wasn't afraid to tell even the silliest of stories. Like the one that involved a horse in a production with the Ballet Russe. From my own experience, I know that having animals onstage never ends well... That night the horse started out with a little gas onstage but made it off before anything catastrophic happened. The backstage area is often very dark during a performance, and the poor horse, who clearly had an upset stomach, left a smelly surprise on the floor offstage. It was hard to detect where the smell was coming from, and with little visibility backstage, one of the dancers, in full costume, ended up facedown in the mess.

Whether through laughter or tears, our conversations felt like a one-on-one master class with a legend. There is a beautiful tradition in ballet that is an innate part of the culture where steps, experiences, and knowledge are passed down from generation to generation, but what Raven and I shared was different. Those experiences with coaches at ABT never extended beyond the studio, and none of them were Black. Raven took that beautiful and rich tradition of teaching and made it feel tailored to me. It was more than passed-down choreography or insight into a role. It was her empathy and compassion that allowed me to feel secure enough to trust and confide in her. She could do this by making me laugh or by casually placing her hand on my knee, letting me know in subtle ways that she understood me.

Raven seamlessly helped bridge the gap for me between Misty the person and Misty the ballerina. As a dancer I've always felt right at home on the stage. There's a sense of safety I feel having complete control over the choices I make and the freedom I feel during a performance that I didn't always possess when I stepped off the stage. Growing up insecure and ashamed that we lived in a motel and were on food stamps, it was often hard for me to connect with people, especially people who I felt judged me or made me feel different. But Raven was that missing piece that helped me to connect the power I felt onstage to the power I held off it. She did this in the most beautiful and clear way that, for me, as a visual learner, made complete sense. She led by example. She was free of judgment, patient and warm. Raven's mastery lay in her ability to give of herself through her loving actions and words. It was as if Raven was determined to pour all the energy that she could no longer expend on her own performing career into helping me with mine.

Early one morning I'd walked my usual seven-block route to the Met from home for company ballet class. This particular morning, as I stood on the corner of Amsterdam Avenue and Sixty-Fifth Street, waiting for the light to change, I noticed the groups of teenagers as they entered the big glass doors of LaGuardia High School, the elite performing arts public high school steps away from Lincoln Center. There were budding musicians holding instrument cases, aspiring artists with portfolios tucked under their arms, and clusters of "bunheads," with erect posture and turned-out feet. It was always inspiring to see a new generation of young dreamers. As I watched them, I hoped to one day be the sort of mentor Raven was becoming for me. I was only beginning to understand the vital importance of someone like her in an artist's life.

The light changed, and I ran across the street and entered the parking garage that led to the Metropolitan Opera House stage door. I checked in at the security desk with my personal ID card, the same one I'd had since I was nineteen years old. The picture was unchanged, and the ABT logo had almost completely faded away. I opened the door that led backstage and stopped at the podium that holds the daily sign-in sheet to write my initials before walking down the long corridor leading to the dressing rooms and the stage. The fluorescent lights overhead flickered, and my heels clicked on the scuffed linoleum floors as I passed the familiar row of lockers used by the Met orchestra. This was the most unglamorous part of this majestic opera house. But after ten years, I felt a pride and a comfort in walking this hall as an insider and veteran.

I paused to look at the announcement boards opposite the lockers. One featured the daily rehearsal schedule. Next to it was a board with the weekly casting, as we alternated ballets once a week. The title read "Casting: Princess Florine." This is a significant role danced by both principals and soloists in *Sleeping Beauty*, which, next to *Swan Lake*, is one of the most iconic classical ballets choreographed by the legendary Marius Petipa, the godfather of epic story ballets, and set to the music of Tchaikovsky. My eyes traveled down the list of names. As I reached the bottom, my heart sank.

Seven women were cast in the role, some of them still members of the corps de ballet. All the female soloists had been cast...except me. By then I'd been a soloist for four years. I'd gotten great reviews so far that season and had danced roles comparable to Princess Florine in other ballets. I'd given everything I knew how to give. Kevin, the rest of the artistic staff, and the choreographers had given me such great feedback about my performances. Alexei Ratmansky told me I was the best Milkmaid he'd ever cast in *The Bright Stream*.

But most importantly, Raven, who'd danced with some of the "greatest of all time," had gushed over my performances. She was my biggest fan and extremely complimentary of my acting and character portrayal. Yet I seemed to be standing still within ABT. I certainly was not getting any closer to my ultimate dream: making it to principal dancer. At that moment, I remembered what Raven had told me just days before. In her soft, yet strong voice, she insisted that no matter how hard the road got, no matter how much it seemed that a career as a classical ballerina would not happen for her, no matter how many times she was told "no" or "it's not possible," she pushed through the adversity on the strength of having hope and faith that with hard work, all things are possible.

The company's casting decisions are cloaked in a kind of

mystery that surrounds the choosing of a pope. Kevin and his second-in-command at the time, Victor Barbee, usually made the casting choices in consultation with the ballet coaches. But Kevin, as artistic director, has the final say. It is a very personal decision. But when an outside choreographer comes in to create a new work, they might see something in you and request you. And this almost always happened with me.

When it came to the full-length classical ballets that were in ABT's repertoire, there were no auditions for roles. You had to be picked. Once again, when it came to a pure classical role, I had not been chosen. This action spoke more loudly than any praise the artistic leadership team had given me. As I walked down the long hallway, my thoughts raced back to the budding artists from LaGuardia. I wanted to be able to tell them, like Raven told me, "All things are possible with hard work." But would I be lying? Was I lying to myself? Would any Black ballerina ever shatter ABT's glass ceiling?

That's the emotional space I was in as I reached the end of the hallway. I stopped just before the artistic staff's offices to collect myself; then I rounded the corner, entering the next hallway that led right to the dressing rooms. I needed to switch off the negative thoughts because thinking this way wouldn't enhance my dancing. Like many dancers of color before me, I had to tune out my pain and fear and tuck it away in order to perform at my best. Over time, the constant need to compartmentalize chips away at your spirit and drains your energy. I took a few deep breaths, swallowed my disappointment and frustration, and headed to the dressing room to get ready for company class.

That night I called Raven. "Hello," she answered. Just hearing her warm, rich voice soothed me.

"Raven, it's Misty."

"How are you?" she asked. I could hear the joy in her voice and hesitated for a moment to share my bad news. "Misty?" she prompted, the tone in her voice indicating she sensed a problem.

"I'm not doing so well," I admitted.

"Tell me everything," she insisted.

And so, I did. I explained it all and shared my complete discouragement.

"Well, that *is* very disappointing," she responded calmly, "and it's not right." Just this affirmation from an artist of her stature, a ballerina who *knew* and had suffered more than I could imagine, was a relief.

"I think you need to go and speak to Kevin," she advised.

I froze in fear. "I don't know if I can do that," I stammered.

"Why not?" Raven asked gently.

"Because...I...I've never *asked* him for a role."

Without hesitation, she enlightened me. "I'm certain others have." Raven spoke firmly from her personal experiences with backstage politics in the ballet world. "What do you have to lose?" she asked simply. I had no answer.

Although Kevin was, at his core, a benevolent man, as dancers, we *all* lived in fear of the power he held over our careers.

And ABT, like every other ballet company, was *not* a democracy. Many of us, including me, didn't challenge decisions made by our artistic leadership. We accepted them and walked to our marks.

"It's not disrespectful to go to your artistic director and let him know what your aspirations are and ask him why you weren't cast when you have danced roles that prove you are up to this one," Raven explained matter-of-factly. As gentle and kind as she was, there were moments when Raven revealed the steeliness that had made her journey possible. This was one of them. Her definitive tone indicated to me that the time for action had come. I knew she was right.

"You sound like Olu; he used to say things like that to me," I confessed.

"I knew I liked him. He's a very wise young man. You should listen to both of us," she teased. "Don't be afraid," she added. "Remember, *when* you go speak to Kevin, I'll be the wind at your back." And I knew she would be.

After we hung up, I thought about Raven at nineteen, auditioning for the all-white Ballet Russe de Monte Carlo in 1955. She had studied at the prestigious Swoboda School, under Maria Swoboda herself, since the age of nine. The Ballet Russe de Monte Carlo had just taken over the school. Though Raven had been a standout student, one of Madame Swoboda's favorites, she'd auditioned twice for the company and been rejected. She was going in for a third time when another dancer warned her, "You really shouldn't. They can't take you. They tour in the South. You're Colored. It's never going to happen." Raven knew the fellow dancer was offering this advice out of concern, not competitive spirit. She appreciated his wanting to protect her, but she was not ready to give up on her dream. She'd enrolled at Columbia University, in the tradition of her educated family, but her heart was at the ballet studio. "The least I could do was try," Raven thought.[1] And so she did. The Wilkinsons were strivers, not quitters.

On the appointed day, she went to the rehearsal studio on West Fifty-Seventh Street, where the school and company were located. She was auditioning for the head of the company, Sergei Denham himself. Mr. Denham was a Russian-born banker who had fled the Communist Revolution. Like Raven, he'd fallen in love with ballet as a child, when he saw the Imperial Ballet perform. In 1945, he'd taken over leadership of this company, which was an offshoot of the original Ballet Russe founded by former members of Sergei Diaghilev's company.

A distinguished man who always wore custom-made suits, Denham sat in his folding chair waiting for the dancers to begin. After watching them take ballet class—a class led by none other than Freddie Franklin[2]—for an hour and a half, he asked to see the dancers one by one. Raven was up. In his thick Russian accent, he asked, "Darling, how would you like to join the Ballet Russe de Monte Carlo?" Raven nearly fell over and accepted joyfully.

He warned her that there could be problems when the company toured in the South, where segregation was still the law of the land. She insisted she could handle the challenge.

"You're not very dark," he commented. "If you took a Russian name, we wouldn't have to admit that you are Colored."

As many who were fortunate to get to know Raven came to understand, Raven never denied being a Black woman, even if it meant costing her the opportunity to dance. "Mr. Denham, I can't deny what I am. How can I dance with my whole self if I do?" she asked him.

"Fair enough," he said. "But don't advertise it."

She told him she wouldn't talk to the press, but "if someone asks me, I have to be honest," Raven insisted. Mr. Denham accepted her stance but later tried to persuade her parents, who were equally firm. No one was going to pressure the Wilkinsons into denying their heritage, which they carried with pride.

As I have so many times since then, I thought of the obstacles Raven overcame when I faced challenges of my own. However great my struggle might be, Raven's had been even harder and, at times, could have cost her life. "The least I could do was try." Her words rang in my head. If she could, and because she had, then I must.

So, a few days after our talk, I went to see Kevin in his cramped temporary office, which sat at the end of the infamous hallway at the Met, where we took up residence for eight weeks. We sat opposite each other. Growing up as a shy, quiet girl in a large family, I was never great at communicating my thoughts verbally. Although I was slowly evolving by having incredible support in my life, like Raven and Olu, that part of me still struggled.

Kevin opened the conversation asking very simply what was on my mind. Sitting up as tall as I could, I began, "The role of Princess Florine."

He asked, confused, "Yes?"

Summoning my courage, I blurted out, "I'm not cast in it."

"Aren't you?" he countered.

"No, I'm not."

"But you danced it before, last season," he affirmed.

"No, I didn't, Kevin," I declared gently but firmly.

"I could have sworn..." He trailed off.

As Kevin searched his memory, I punctured the silence. "Is there a reason I wasn't cast? Because I know I can do it."

"Of course you can. There's no reason. It's just...an oversight," he explained.

I was gobsmacked by his response. How many "oversights" had there been? I wondered. Was this the first? Or had there been others? It made me feel somewhat forgotten and was a clear reminder that my career was no one's priority but my own. As Black dancers, we're often told that we don't blend in visually. Even worse was feeling completely overlooked.

I composed myself and let him know that I had never performed the role of Princess Florine, let alone been given the opportunity to understudy and learn the role, a common practice for dancers to gain experience and prepare them for the possibility of performing it in the future. "There are corps dancers performing the part," I pointed out. "As a soloist, I think I should be dancing it."

"Well, let me see if I can find a date," Kevin reassured me. "I'm glad you came to see me about this."

"Thank you for seeing me," I offered, and walked out of his office.

A few days later, after signing in, I walked past the casting board, and there was my name under Princess Florine, "Matinee: June 9, 2011." The long, dingy corridor had never felt more welcoming. Raven had been right about communicating directly. I'd spoken to Kevin and had been cast in the role. That night I called her. "We did it," I said breathlessly.

"No," she answered, "*you* did it." But I knew that I'd borrowed my courage from her mighty heart.

Everything Is Beautiful at the Ballet

Raven's career with the Ballet Russe de Monte Carlo began shortly after her successful audition with a series of performances at the prestigious Lyric Opera House in Chicago. Sergei Denham, the director of the company, used this out-of-town engagement as a "tryout," though he didn't admit this to Raven directly. At twenty years old, Raven was innocent but not naive. She understood immediately that she was being tested. She didn't tell her parents that she hadn't yet received a formal contract because she didn't want to worry them. The Wilkinsons fully supported her aspiration, but they had concerns about its viability given the highly competitive nature of dance and the racial realities of America in 1955. Like any loving parents, they didn't want their daughter's spirit to be crushed.[3] It's unlikely that Mr. Denham doubted Raven's artistic ability, which he had witnessed firsthand in her audition and which his star dancers,

Freddie Franklin and Alexandra Danilova, had enthusiastically endorsed. But since the Ballet Russe was a touring company, Denham wanted to see if Raven's presence in the company would cause concerns.

The company completed their stay at the Opera House without any unwelcome attention. Extremely pleased, Denham offered Raven a contract as soon as they had finished. Though she'd been raised to be very polite, and it was a time when, as Raven used to say, "little girls were to be seen and not heard," she let Mr. Denham know that she was fully aware he'd put her "on trial" because of her race.[4] That was so typical of the Raven I was beginning to know. Without being abrasive, she let people know she understood their motives, and she couldn't be played for a fool. As someone who has taken several years to find her voice and advocate for herself, I am continually amazed and motivated by Raven's "steel spine," even when she was a very young dancer.

Raven always described her first two years in the Ballet Russe de Monte Carlo as free of strife. In October 1955, *Dance News* announced that she and six other dancers had joined the company with a candid group photograph. The article never mentioned her race.[5] Raven had kept her word to Denham that she would not broadcast her identity to the press, to avoid "causing problems."

Normally, an achievement such as hers, being the first Black woman to join the most prestigious touring ballet company in the world, would have landed her on the front page of one of the nation's many Black newspapers like the *Chicago Defender* or New York's *Amsterdam News*. But Mr. Denham had made clear to Raven and her family that the repercussions of publicizing this breakthrough would not be good, neither for the Ballet Russe nor for her as a ballerina. Segregation was the law of the land in the South and an accepted social practice in the North. Like most directors of majority arts organizations at the time, Mr. Denham did not want to invite controversy or publicly engage in the civil rights battles that were brewing across America.

Over the years, I have heard people imply that Raven was "passing" in order to preserve her career because she wasn't shouting "I am Black" from the rooftops. She always insisted that when asked, she never lied and that she had the right to work and travel first and foremost "as an artist and a human being." She was also following her mother's lifelong teachings. The dark-haired, olive-complexioned Mrs. Wilkinson would often be asked, "What are you? Are you Spanish?" She would invariably answer, "I'm an American," and she instructed her children to do the same.

In a culture that has often treated African Americans as "aliens" who should be "shipped back to the continent from which they were originally brought," Mrs. Wilkinson's statement was a declaration of Black rights to full citizenship. Raven was nothing if not proud of her heritage, but like many Black pioneers of her era, she walked a tightrope and had to balance the desire to "say it loud" against succeeding in a field that was closed to her people, thereby forging a path for others. She belonged to a generation that led with proof of excellence first and identity second. This may be hard for people today to grasp. But even now, when I speak of my identity as a Black woman in ballet, there are those who accuse me of "playing the race card." Even in the twenty-first century, there are people who don't appreciate being reminded that my experiences differ from theirs and that I've faced greater obstacles.

Even if America wasn't quite prepared to integrate in 1955, the members of the Ballet Russe were. Raven's fellow company members, who came from around the country, as well as from South America and Russia, embraced her. When Raven first joined, legendary ballerina Eleanor D'Antuono was a wide-eyed fifteen-year-old corps de ballet member from a doting family in Cambridge, Massachusetts. She described seeing Raven for the very first time in ballet class at the Fifty-Seventh Street studio. "I had never seen a more elegant person, educated and elegant...No one in the company had ever been that elegant and that poised," Eleanor stated emphatically in a recent conversation we had. "I called my mother and said, 'That's who I'd like to be my roommate. Do you think she would consider it?'"

Eleanor's mother encouraged her to ask the twenty-year-old. After their first rehearsal together, a shy Eleanor approached Raven, who accepted the offer to room together during tours. From then on, the two petite, dark-haired ballerinas were inseparable, eating all their meals together and sitting next to each other on the bus that carried the company from city to city, town to town. Eleanor's admiration for Raven extended to her dancing, which to this day she describes as "so refined...It was like seeing Margot Fonteyn. I just wanted to be close and learn from her." She also pointed out a feature many have noted: Raven's exquisite feet, which is significant because Black dancers have historically been told that our bodies are not suited to ballet, with "flat feet" being held up as the purported evidence.

Every year, from October through April, the Ballet Russe traveled across the country. Their destinations included big cities like Chicago, Atlanta, Los Angeles, and San Francisco, and small towns in the North and the South. At the time, every town in America boasted some version of an opera house because the art form had been very popular in the late nineteenth century. Ballet was still new to most American audiences, and Raven and her fellow dancers played to standing-room-only crowds.

Sometimes they'd stay in a place for just one night, or they'd arrive at eight in the morning and have to get off the bus and run straight to rehearsal. Raven and I often compared notes on our touring experiences. I could relate to the pressure of hitting the ground running hours after landing someplace. And ABT's travels around the world with eighty dancers packed into the plane of one of our sponsoring airlines seems very similar to Raven's descriptions of the Ballet Russe troupe packed into a bus, desperately catching up on rest by sleeping on the way. Mr. Denham insisted that the ballerinas all wear skirts to travel so they would look "ladylike" upon arrival, much like what we see today when college and professional athletes arrive in a city, dressed in business attire, before suiting up to compete in their seasonal games.

We settled easily into conversations about rehearsing for and performing similar repertoire, including great classics like *Swan Lake*, *The Nutcracker* (in which Raven often danced the Chinese Tea pas de deux), *Gaîté Parisienne*, *Raymonda*, and *Don Quixote*. She also pirouetted down memory lane when recalling performances of *Scheherazade*, as well as some pieces that have not stood the test of time, like *La Dame à la Licorne*, with a story by the great French dramatist and filmmaker Jean Cocteau.

I happily spent hours listening closely as Raven raved about the extraordinary dance luminaries she met and worked with: the Cuban prima ballerina Alicia Alonso; Maria Tallchief, who rehearsed them in Ballet Imperial; and, of course, Freddie Franklin, whom I also had the pleasure of knowing. But it was from Ms. Alonso that Raven confided she learned the most about performance.

Ms. Alonso would spend hours explaining to the dancers how to achieve true artistry. During one tour, she took over rehearsals of *Swan Lake* and *Giselle*. She taught the dancers that, as Raven put it, "there was a whole world of being onstage beyond just doing the steps." She encouraged the dancers to think about who their characters were before they stepped out in front of the audience. "You are playing Giselle's friend. How are you with your friends?" Alonso challenged them.

Raven soaked it all in, saying, "I was in a college of ballet." Though Ms. Alonso had an eye condition leaving her partially blind, Raven relished the fact that she caught every error. "She couldn't see anything, but she always saw what we did," she would say with a laugh. Just watching Ms. Alonso perform was, for Raven, an education in excellence. She said that Alonso's interpretation of Giselle's "mad scene," the famous scene where the character Giselle goes mad after she realizes that the man she's fallen in love with is engaged to another woman, brought her to tears.[6]

I can understand how Alicia Alonso, in even the most subtle ways, was a great teacher and influence. I had met Ms. Alonso on a couple of occasions, along with the rest of the ABT dancers over the years. But I had the privilege of meeting Ms. Alonso in November 2016 in a much more intimate setting. I had completed my first spring and fall seasons with ABT as a principal dancer. It was an extremely emotional time for me because at that point I was still battling within myself over whether I belonged. Having the title of principal dancer does not reverse nearly fifteen years of challenges around fitting in, being "the only" or one of the only, or even working to meet your own expectations. Those feelings were still there. But Raven's wisdom and strength taught me to never let the frustration of being an "only" discourage me. Being given an opportunity to make it possible for doors to be opened for others made me work harder every day, reminding me that nothing had been given to me. Like others who were promoted to principal dancer, I, too, had earned it.

Going to Cuba as an ambassador of the United States under President Barack Obama's US Department of State was an honor. I knew it was going to be a busy trip—seeing Cuban dance companies perform and speaking with their dancers, meeting various dignitaries, and having dinner each night at a restaurant. Everyone I met during my trip carried so much love and a sense of community. But it was the chance to take company class at the Cuban National Ballet, which was founded by Ms. Alonso in 1948 in Havana, that has stayed with me all these years.

Then a spry ninety-five-year-old, Ms. Alonso was still a regular presence at the company and school, and she made sure to be on-site while my small group was there. Ms. Alonso, in her dark sunglasses, draped in a beautiful sea of lilac and purple hues, including the scarf that elegantly covered her head, called me into her office, where she spoke in warm whispers with me. She knew I was preparing for my debut as Giselle at the Met for the 2017 season. Her advice for me, much like Raven's recollections of Ms. Alonso, was very simple but just what I needed in that moment. "Misty, be strong, confident, and remember to smile when you dance Giselle." I held back tears as she spoke because I didn't want to miss a single word of what she offered to me as we embraced.

The day before we were to leave Cuba, the US Embassy threw a small gathering for us at their compound to bid us farewell. A young man rushed into the space, slightly out of breath. In fact, he'd arrived with a gift from Ms. Alonso for me, and he was afraid that he might not catch me before I left the embassy. It was her parting gift to me, a DVD of her Giselle performance with a handwritten note wishing me luck on my forthcoming performance and again, "Remember to smile."

It's a big honor when a true master takes the time to see and encourage you. Alicia Alonso had done that for both Raven and me, and although generations apart as dancers, that connection is one we uniquely share. I was excited to hear more from Raven about all that she learned on the road with the Ballet Russe and their United Nations of dancers. Although she had experience dancing in the studio for most of her life, at the end of the day, to really soar as an artist, you have to perform live. And that's the fulfillment and experience she got from being on tour.

When you are so entrenched in this art form, it's often easy to forget the incredible impact it can have on an audience. When I started touring and performing with ABT, it gave me a whole new perspective on the transformative power of ballet. Raven described experiencing this during one of her very first tours. It was the middle of her first year, and she and the other dancers were completely exhausted after a long string of "one-nighters." They were in a tiny town, performing *The Nutcracker*. Though Raven loved her work, it was one of those performances she'd really had to get her energy up for because every muscle in her body ached, and all she wanted was a full meal and a warm bed. The theater was small enough that she could see the audience's faces from the stage, which in a large opera house is not the case.

As she looked out, she saw expressions of absolute wonder and joy. The audience was mesmerized by what seemed to them to be pure magic unfolding onstage. From that moment, Raven learned never to underestimate the privilege it was to inspire such awe and amazement in an audience.[7] Raven's abundance of gratitude was always in the back of my mind on days when it was difficult to get out of bed or rehearse a role I'd done many times before. With insights like this, she always reminded me that every performance is a gift to the audience, and we should cherish each step. Her glee in recounting these experiences also taught me that seeing a performance could change a person's life. In sharing her memories, and by her example, Raven showed me how to dance with greater intent, knowing that I was communicating with every single audience member.

The Nutcracker experience gave Raven renewed vigor in her grueling schedule. She described those early years in the company as heavenly and everything she'd dreamed about being an artist. She and Eleanor would even go to dinner in between shows in most cities, usually for hamburgers or steaks, with no problems.

Yet the dangers that lay ahead were foreshadowed by one incident at a hotel in Georgia. Because they were in the South, Raven and Eleanor decided to order room service. A Black waiter wheeled in a tray of their favorites: burgers and french fries. As he lifted the covers off the plates, he stared very hard at Raven. A slightly tense silence ensued as she and Eleanor exchanged nervous glances. Finally, he asked, "What nationality are you?" Eleanor was about to jump in with "I'm Italian and she's—" But Raven, knowing exactly why he was asking, cut Eleanor off. Maintaining the calm her mother had taught her, she said, "We are American. What are you?" Whether he understood her plight or not, the waiter decided not to press the issue further and left them to have their meal in peace.[8]

Despite what was bubbling under the surface offstage, onstage Raven was thriving. Her dancing was so exquisite that within eighteen months of joining the company, she was promoted to soloist, a remarkably fast ascent in the ballet world. One of the plum roles she was given was the waltz solo in *Les Sylphides*, a principal role that would become her signature. She was partnered by white men in a time when mixed couples were banned from television screens. Though I've never seen footage of Raven dancing this ballet, I can imagine it from the photographs of her that depict the quintessential ethereal ballerina. What's even more astonishing is that Black women to this day are rarely cast as the lead in *Les Sylphides* or other ballets from the romantic genre because we're told we aren't soft or ethereal enough. Raven was making history.

Those first two years in the company were among the happiest and artistically satisfying of Raven's life. She was developing into the ballerina she'd worked so hard to be, flourishing among her newfound colleagues, and enjoying the adventurous life of a young "artist and human being" on the road. Within months, this season of peace would come to an end.

Raven's fulfilling experience dancing with the Ballet Russe in those early years without focus on her race reminded me of my own early experience in ballet, a time when all that seemed to matter was my talent. When I started dancing, I was immediately called a prodigy. I was given a contract to join ABT's Studio Company with only four years of ballet training under my belt. It wasn't until I became a member of ABT's corps de ballet that the color of my skin entered the discussion, at least to my knowledge. Behind the scenes some of the artistic staff questioned whether I should be cast in the "ballet blanc" productions when they were being filmed, or as it translates to, "white ballet." This is a nineteenth-century romantic style that typically consists of supernatural creatures and spirits dressed in all white and danced by a body of white dancers. They were afraid that I would distract from the uniformity when an entire corps de ballet is white, something generations of Black ballerinas have experienced.

What was frustrating was the lack of belief or understanding from my peers. When I would point out the discrimination in the art form, they would brush it off with a smile and say, "We just see you as our Misty. We don't see you as Black." And yet, as I watched the other Black dancers, all of them men, with whom

I'd joined the company, fall away one by one, I became "the only." My loneliness was acute. I felt less and less like Raven's description of "just a human being and an artist" and more like a test case in whether a Black woman could aspire to make it to the highest levels of a rarefied art form.

CHAPTER 5

TAKING FLIGHT

I began the spring season of 2012 with a heart full of hope as Kevin gave me unprecedented opportunities to show my growth and to further develop my artistry. All the roles I was to debut were leading roles. A first for me. And because they were all lead roles, I knew my performance dates far in advance and could share them with Raven and with Olu, who, although we were not yet back together, attended every single one.

This new responsibility, and the advanced casting that came with it, also afforded me the time to delve more deeply into each of the characters I would be portraying. I used the time to work with a theater coach, who challenged me to bring meaning to every moment of my performances. We worked on every entrance, every reaction, motivation, and backstory. I further began to unpack each character by asking, "Who was this person before she entered the stage?"

I was determined to seize this opportunity and to prove to Kevin, the artistic leadership, and the ballet world—as well as myself—what I could do if only given the chance. With some trepidation, I allowed myself to believe that my biggest dreams, including being promoted one day to principal dancer, just might be in reach. Maybe. Just maybe.

I was cast in the role of *La Bayadère*'s Gamzatti, for which I fought hard, proving myself to iconic ballerina Natalia Makarova, who was setting the ballet on the company. Natalia's opinion overrode Kevin's when deciding the casting for this ballet because this was her production, derived from Chabukiani and Ponomarev's 1941 redaction for the Mariinsky Theatre.

Kevin felt I was ready to take on this role, but Natalia was hesitant and let her skepticism be known. She not only set the ballet but also coached those performing lead roles.

"No, your arms are limp," she'd snap at me in front of everyone. "You are the daughter of the ruler, not some girl next door! Present yourself!"

All her doubts and criticisms drove me and eventually mirrored how I would approach and develop the character of Gamzatti: with strength, will, and determination.

The ballet is set in a royal court in seventeenth-century India. Gamzatti is characterized as the haughty and vindictive princess who tries to poison the young temple dancer from the "wrong side of the tracks" who's stolen her fiancé's heart. The part was technically demanding as well as a phenomenal acting opportunity. I welcomed the challenge.

One of my favorite things about tackling substantive acting roles is finding ways to connect with the character. Offering words of wisdom, Raven encouraged me to understand and feel the grief and reasoning behind a character's actions because it's the best way for an audience to see Gamzatti's humanity and not simply present another "mean girl" interpretation. The challenge was capturing her cruelty while also providing the audience a chance to sympathize with the pain that drove her. And, of course, I was determined to win over my harshest critic: Natalia Makarova.

Besides the role of Gamzatti, I was also selected by Christopher Wheeldon, one of the most sought-after contemporary choreographers, to dance the main pas de deux in his *Thirteen Diversions*, an abstract ballet that was set to the music of Benjamin Britten. Wheeldon's pieces are full of intricate footwork and intense passion. His choreographic and storytelling gifts extend to numerous stages, including the Broadway adaptation of *An American in Paris*, based on the 1951 film starring Gene Kelly and Leslie Caron, for which Wheeldon won a Tony Award for Best Choreography. At that time in my career, getting big opportunities to work with choreographers like Wheeldon in contemporary ballets like *Thirteen Diversions* was key in preparing me to take on principal roles in classical works.

And then there was the jewel in the crown: I was one of three ballerinas selected by Alexei Ratmansky, our artist in residence, to dance the Firebird in his restaging of this groundbreaking ballet, which debuted at the original Ballets Russes, set to a score by Igor Stravinsky.

I'll never forget where I was when I heard about my *Firebird* casting. When ABT's summer hiatus began, I decided to spend my remaining months working with Dance Theatre of Harlem, the company founded in 1969 by Arthur Mitchell (who had become the first African American principal dancer at New York City Ballet in 1956) and Ballet Russe de Monte Carlo alumnus Karel Shook in response to the assassination of Dr. Martin Luther King Jr.

It was during one of our breaks from rehearsing that I happened to open Twitter on my cell phone and see that someone had posted the press release announcing the casting for ABT's forthcoming *Firebird* production. I had been told that I would be learning the role of the Firebird months before, and as exciting as that was, I had been learning lead roles my entire career and had yet to actually be cast. So my expectations were low, though I always maintained a glimmer of hope. I was astonished when I read that I'd been cast. I'd be the first Black woman to perform the title role of the Firebird with ABT.

Tears filled my eyes as I stared at my phone as though the words might disappear if I looked away. And how fitting it was for me to be lovingly surrounded by dancers of color in this historic Black building, artists who looked like me and understood my journey in ballet.

It was especially poignant because *Firebird* was one of DTH's world-renowned signature pieces thanks to trailblazing ballerinas like Stephanie Dabney, Tai Jimenez, Christina Johnson, Kellye Saunders, and Paunika Jones, who transported audiences as they watched each of these extraordinary women bring her Firebird to life on the stage.

Now it would be my turn to make a Firebird of my own interpretation. It was too good to be true. But it was true. I called my manager, Gilda, to share the great news. My voice was so filled with emotion that she could barely understand what I was attempting to say. I finally blurted out, "I'm going to be the Firebird! I'm so happy! I had started to believe this could never happen for me!"

Although Gilda had been working with me as my manager for several months, she admitted often that she was still getting familiar with ballet and its history. She had never heard of *Firebird*, though she didn't tell me that at the time. I could tell she was excited for me, and as we ended the call, she, too, had emotion in her voice and said quietly, "Congratulations. You got this."

Gilda called Raven immediately after we hung up. She wanted to fully understand what this opportunity would mean for me, and who better to ask than a woman who'd seen and heard it all in ballet? "*Which* Firebird in the flock will she be?" Raven wanted to clarify.

Even in 2011, it took Raven a moment to process the news that a ballet that had been debuted by the legendary Sergei Diaghilev, a ballet in which she had danced as a member of the corps of the Ballet Russe de Monte Carlo in the 1950s, would now be *headlined by a Black woman in a white company*. Gilda reassured her, "She's dancing *the* Firebird." It really was a shock to us all, even to Raven, who was the ultimate optimist, especially when it came to my career, that after all this time, a Black woman would hold the title role of *the* featured ballet of ABT's 2012 Metropolitan Opera House season and the most eagerly anticipated restaging of any ballet in a decade.

When I spoke with Raven days later, she couldn't wait to hear the story of how I learned this news. I told her every detail, down to staring at my phone, terrified that I was dreaming that I saw my name as the lead, and then how I was swallowed up in the tight embrace of a group of Black dancers at DTH who swayed with pride as we celebrated the news. Raven and I laughed and cried as we excitedly looked forward to what the coming months would bring.

Before each performance season, ABT produces marketing photo shoots and videos that are used to help promote what is to come throughout the run. Since *Firebird* was a cornerstone of the 2012 Met season, it was no surprise that ABT would include something to highlight the ballet. What was exhilarating was that I was the ballerina chosen to do the shoot as the Firebird.

The photo that resulted from renowned photographer

Fabrizio Ferri showed a confident and strong Black ballerina en pointe. The image draped the front of the Metropolitan Opera House for the entire spring season, and she happened to be me. The first time I saw the image on the Met Opera House, I shed tears of joy because I didn't simply see myself on the front of the Met. I saw a Black woman representing generations of people who never felt welcomed or accepted in that space. But those weren't my only tears shed heading into the season. The growing pain in my leg threatened each day to bring everything I was working for to a halt.

On the surface, it should have been a heady time for me. The road ahead was filled with so much promise. It's the kind of trajectory that professional ballerinas work our whole lives for. But in truth, there were mounting physical *and* mental pressures. I have always embraced the understanding of "When and where I enter, the whole race enters with me." This belief has guided my decisions about how I navigate the world and how I represent myself. I strive to serve as an example of what it means to be a proud Black woman. I try to not allow other people's words and thoughts to define how I see myself. But I am human, and as the 2012 Met season approached, I began to feel less confident in what I could feasibly deliver.

I feared the reaction of critics and the jabs from online commentators that maybe I wasn't "right" for these leading roles. Like anyone with a public profile in the digital age, I was on the receiving end of my fair share of hate posts. The more I accomplished in the ballet world, the more it felt like walking a tightrope over a large crowd, half of which cheered me on, the other half of which couldn't wait to see me fall.

Those fears were exacerbated by the pain in my shin that had begun to worsen throughout the year heading into the spring season. At its worst, it felt like being stabbed with a steak knife. After an icing, it would subside, and I worked through it. As a dancer or an athlete, you're taught to "play hurt." So, I did my best to deny the pain. But after every icing wore off, those stabs returned, sharper, refusing to be ignored.

I purposely kept my dilemma quiet for fear of being pulled out of the season. If I did not find a way to push through, I might never get another chance. I called Raven often, just to talk. It was inevitable that I would tell her what I was going through because the Met season was only a few weeks away. As a retired ballerina who'd endured her own fair share of pain and injury, she understood fully the extent of what I might be facing, especially with a role like the Firebird, which required quite a lot of jumping. Every impact my pointe shoe made with the stage in rehearsals and performances meant potential further damage to what was clearly a mounting problem.

Rather than *discourage* me or tell me what might not happen, Raven, instead, *encouraged* me to be honest with my body and take the time I needed to rest as much as possible. She called to speak with me on a near-daily basis, just to ask how I was feeling and if I was taking care of myself as she'd instructed. Although

I was following her advice to the best of my ability, she and I both knew how difficult it would be to take the care I needed when working toward a full performance season that could be career-defining.

Somehow, I got through my performances of *La Bayadère* as Gamzatti. The pain, by this point, was nonstop, and the affected area of my shin had begun to swell. No amount of icing, acupuncture, or massage was able to help. I kept my focus on the days ahead to my *Firebird* performance. Raven attended one of my *La Bayadère* performances, and after the show she walked quietly alongside me as we made our way to our respective homes from the theater.

"How is your pain, Misty? Tell me honestly," she asked gently.

"It's not good. It's constant and I have no idea how I'm going to get through this performance, Raven."

"You're under a lot of pressure. If you just calm your mind and focus on enjoying yourself, maybe the pain and stress will subside…"

"Maybe you're right," I replied, only half believing her.

"But tonight you danced beautifully. You were a regal Gamzatti. The way you extended your neck and chin and those beautiful arms. I couldn't wait for you to return to the stage to see what you'd give us next. You were magnificent."

I thanked Raven for always being a genuine champion for me, mostly because I knew that she understood intimately what I was working toward. Before we parted ways that night, I smiled when I told Raven, "Someone else agrees that I performed a great Gamzatti."

"Who else might that be?" Raven asked, eager to know.

"Natalia Makarova. When I came off the stage after taking my bows, she told me, 'Misty, you *are* a queen.'" That's an example of the highest praise from Ms. Makarova. Raven beamed. "NOW we know she has taste!" she exclaimed. Those tranquil moments walking with Raven into the summer New York City night, along with her and Natalia Makarova's positive feedback, helped carry me through some of the most physically demanding days of my career to date as we counted down to the New York premiere of *Firebird*.

The night of my performance of *Firebird* coincided with Kevin McKenzie's twentieth anniversary as artistic director. That evening, the Metropolitan Opera House welcomed one of the most racially diverse audiences the ballet had ever attracted. People of color from every walk of life and from all over the country came, all in support of a Black woman dancing the title role. There were fathers in suits escorting their beribboned little girls decked out in their Sunday best, young couples, groups of women who'd come by bus from Philadelphia, several current and past dancers from DTH, and many Black patrons and supporters from New York's influential and philanthropic community. I hoped that night would open the doors for a new audience to feel welcome at the Met theater and to continue to come see ABT beyond that performance.

I remember seeing photos of the lines outside the Met from the front doors as far back as the fountain in the middle of Lincoln Center, all of them waiting to get inside the opera house. It was incredibly exciting, not just for the people who came to see the performance, but for me, too. First, however, I had to actually take the stage and soar as the Firebird. I prayed that my leg would sustain me through all the jumping the role required me to do.

When I am completely present and in the moment of a performance, I don't always remember every detail of what happened, as if I black out and come to when the show has ended. But the standing ovations at the curtain call reassured me that it had been a success. I allowed myself to feel pride in giving my all. After the performance, there was a champagne reception onstage with special guests, company members, trustees, and supporters. It was magical to stand onstage, looking out at the massive, empty opera house, the rows and rows of red velvet seats that only minutes before had been filled with nearly four thousand cheering audience members.

Many of my good friends stayed for the reception, including the writer and film director Nelson George, who was interested in directing a documentary about my career. That night, I introduced him to Raven, who instantly charmed him, as she did everyone she ever met. I watched as Nelson's wheels turned, and it became clear that night that Raven would play a prominent role in any film George made about me. He was enthralled by our parallel journeys as Black ballerinas, set apart by half a century, and the fact that Raven was seeing the results of the path she helped create, which made my dancing on that stage possible.

Raven was in her glory, talking to *everyone*: the stagehands, the dancers, the special guests, the children of the special guests. She also made certain to take me aside to share her thoughts on my performance. She was so proud of the season overall. But most of all, she couldn't believe how I had danced the role of the Firebird, becoming the creature who frees all the women being held captive by an evil sorcerer.

"Misty, you became a bird tonight. The way you moved your arms, the tap-tap flickering of your feet, the rapid head movements from side to side...I didn't see you up there. I saw a Firebird."

Listening to her, I was reminded that, by dancing that role, I was setting other Black women free to dance, to dream big, to "fly." It felt like more than a coincidence that the same year Raven officially stepped away from the stage, she danced directly into my life. I felt as though she was meant to come into my life to pass me the torch and guide me at such a critical point in my career. The climb from soloist to principal can be steep, and many never make it. And no Black woman had ever been promoted to that level at ABT. Furthermore, it was still rare to find a Black woman principal dancer at any of the major classical ballet companies. Lauren Anderson was the first to be promoted to principal dancer in 1990 at Houston Ballet, and in 2006, Tai Jimenez joined Boston Ballet as a principal dancer.

What Raven said next stopped me in my tracks: she told me that given how I'd tackled *Firebird*, she could absolutely see me dancing Odette/Odile in *Swan Lake*. Odette/Odile was the *ultimate* ballet role. I often felt like bowing to Raven, but when she said this, I wanted to fall to my knees and thank her. I didn't, because we were surrounded by other people, and she would have died of embarrassment. I also didn't because the pain in my shin, the pain I'd ignored and worked "in spite of" since before the beginning of the season, had now become excruciating.

No one really noticed, but I could barely stand. But that performance was my way of showing gratitude. I wanted to thank not only Raven but also the Black community. I wanted to thank them for their investment in me and my performances all season and particularly for the way they showed up that night and for making clear what the evening, and dancing the role of the Firebird, symbolized. I had to perform and represent for them—for us—no matter the pain I was in—to give possibilities to past, present, and future generations of Black people that night. This is what it was all for.

But Raven noticed me wince. "What's wrong?" she asked, instinctively knowing my happy demeanor masked pain and fear.

"It's my shin," I admitted. "It's killing me."

I was trying to underplay the gravity, but as usual, she saw through me. "It's time, Misty. You must see your doctor." She insisted. I promised I would, though I was terrified what that visit might reveal. It was easier to live with the pain and be in denial. Raven took my hand and reassured me, "You're going to be all right. And you're going to dance all the great roles. NOTHING can stop you now," she insisted. I wanted to believe her, but the discomfort reminded me that the road to my dreams had always been full of bumps, obstacles, and major setbacks. As joyous as the night was, I had the sinking feeling that I was going to be tested yet again. Why had I even allowed myself to get carried away by hope?

The exhilarating highs, followed by crashing lows, are part of any dancer's journey, given the potential for injury and the nature of the art form, where dozens are competing for a few major roles. We are all at the mercy of our bodies and of the tastes and whims of our artistic directors. I'd seen many rising stars come crashing to the ground in my eleven years with ABT. The fear that I might end up as one of them was never far from my mind. On top of the universal possibility of injury, many Black women before me had attempted to reach the pinnacle in ballet, and their dreams had been shattered by the realities of race in dance and in America. Reflecting on Raven's path usually inspired me with hope. But in vulnerable moments like this one, I was more susceptible to letting doubt creep in; the trials she endured reminded me of the limitations on the career of a Black ballerina. And left me wondering what it would take to truly overcome.

Even still, Raven's journey was fraught with much more than the normal pain and injury of a dancer. Her career with the Ballet Russe had been derailed by forces that wanted to do more than just prevent her from advancing; they quite literally wanted to destroy her.

Burning Crosses

Racial tensions were rising throughout the country as the civil rights movement gained steam. Brown v. the Board of Education had struck down "separate but equal" education in 1954. Emmett Till's murder in 1955 awakened the entire nation to the horrors of lynching and vigilante violence. The Montgomery Bus Boycott, which lasted from 1955 to 1956, led to the Browder v. Gayle decision, affirmed by the Supreme Court, that declared bus segregation was unconstitutional. Faced with these disruptions of a long-accepted way of life, the South began doubling down on Jim Crow. The state of Virginia shut down its public schools rather than let Black children and white children attend together, a strategy known as "massive resistance." Violence against Black people who "didn't know their place" increased.

Raven's days of touring the South without incident came to an abrupt end. The peace she had known in her first two years with the Ballet Russe was soon to be shattered. The first inkling came during a tour stop in Atlanta, Georgia, in 1957. The company arrived at the hotel in which they'd stayed two years before. Realizing that the atmosphere was tense and the reality on the ground was shifting, the company manager decided to have her roommate, Eleanor, sign in for their room while Raven was whisked upstairs with other dancers. Hours after arriving, Raven and the manager were summoned to the front desk. Eleanor, always at Raven's side, insisted on joining them. When the dancers had first arrived, the hotel manager had asked the company manager if they had a Black person among them. He had lied and said no. Still suspicious, since he knew the company from a prior visit, the hotel manager asked the elevator operator, a Black woman, if she had seen a "Colored dancer," and the woman immediately identified Raven.

Raven, Eleanor, and the company manager now stood at the front desk.

"You're Colored, aren't you?" the manager asked point-blank.

"Yes, sir, I am," Raven stated, with her back straight and looking him dead in the eye.

"Well, then, miss, I'm sorry, but you can't stay here. You'll have to go to the Colored hotel."

"That's outrageous!" Eleanor cried, incensed.

"Isn't there another solution?" the company manager implored.

"Why are you kicking me out?" Raven finally interjected calmly. "When I stayed here only two years ago, there was no problem. Why was I able to stay then?"

"I know you did. I remember," the manager admitted, embarrassed.

"You even checked me in," she reminded the manager.

"I sure did. And I am so sorry. But things are different now. With this civil rights business, it's gotten hot around here. Folks don't like what's happening. They want us to stick to the rules. The way they were. Not the new rules. If you stay here, they're liable to bomb the place," the manager explained.

Incredibly, every time I heard Raven share this story, she had sympathy and compassion for the hotel manager. She could see how much he hated kicking her out, as well as his genuine terror. She would always say, "I didn't want to put anyone in danger." In all the horrific and terrifying situations she faced in the South, her concern for her fellow dancers and the people around her was always greater than her fears for herself. She never expressed anger at the elevator operator who had "outed" her, either. Raven understood better than anyone I've ever met how racism traps everyone in a no-win situation, bringing out the worst in all of us. Her response was always to rise to her best self. She was the embodiment of "Be the change you want to see in the world."

So rather than put up more of a fight, Raven said to the hotel manager, who by that time was sweating with anxiety and pleading with her to leave:

"Very well. I'll go. I don't want anyone to be hurt because of me."

"Thank you so much, miss. And I truly am sorry. We'll get you a taxi right away. Thank you."

"Where are they taking you?" Eleanor asked, horrified and incredulous at the scene she was witnessing: her best friend, the most elegant woman she'd ever met, was being banished from the hotel where the entire company was staying. Eleanor by this time had met Raven's family, shared meals at their home. Dr. and Mrs. Wilkinson watched over her like a daughter. She couldn't believe Raven, a soloist in the Ballet Russe, one of its finest dancers, her role model, and the daughter of one of the most magnificent families she'd ever known, was being treated like a pariah. In America. Her own country. The world's greatest democracy.[1]

"If you can't stay here, I'm not staying here!" Eleanor announced defiantly. "I'm going with you."

"You can't," Raven answered softly.

"Why not?" Eleanor asked.

"I'm going to a Colored hotel. It's illegal for you to stay there with me. That's the way it is down here. Don't worry. I'll be all right. And I'll see you at the theater," Raven answered reassuringly, ever the big sister to Eleanor.

And with that, Raven gathered her belongings, got into the Colored taxi that had been called for her, and went across town to the hotel reserved for Black people. That evening, she showed up looking pristine at the theater and did her performance of the waltz in *Les Sylphides* just as she always did, with passion for the Chopin music and the lyrical leaps in her solo.

We dancers are highly sensitive and emotional beings. We have to be in order to bring the power and expressiveness that most roles require. I don't know where Raven stored the pain of those moments and how she managed not to let them affect her performances or break her. All the audience saw in Atlanta that night was a sylph soaring through the air. I learned from Raven that our performances, if we do our jobs, will live forever in those who come to see us dance. That should be the only thing we're thinking about when we're on that stage, how to bring the role to life in a way that is unforgettable and makes the audience see only the character. That's the job. So maybe that was Raven's secret on that night and any night when she experienced the suffocating grips of racism while on the road: Soar above the hate. Lose yourself in the music and the steps, which will live on long after bigotry has died. Defeat hatred with beauty.

As ugly as that experience was, it was just a tiny taste of much worse situations to come.

Raven always said that part of what helped make such humiliations bearable was the unflagging support of the other dancers, who rallied around her. The men would escort her to and from the theater and then escort her and Eleanor to dinner. Everyone in the company was appalled by the ignorance and the hatred they witnessed.

On one trip to Daytona Beach, one of the dancers even had her parents open their home to Raven so she could be safe and comfortable, not relegated to a Colored hotel. Reflecting on it years later, Raven marveled at the parents' willingness to host her. Coming from Florida, they probably harbored the same prejudices other Southerners did, and yet they overcame them to help her.[2]

Not surprisingly, few people demonstrated this type of understanding or even compassion. The South was a tinder-box and the home of state-sanctioned violence and terror. I'll never forget when Raven first shared with me her up-close-and-personal encounter with the Ku Klux Klan while on tour one afternoon in 1957. The Ballet Russe bus rolled into Montgomery, Alabama, home of the bus boycott. Masses of hooded men and women marched on the streets. They blocked the bus's path, bringing it to a halt. Two hooded men boarded the bus, threw pamphlets at the terrified dancers, and then ran off.

Later that day at the hotel, a little rattled, Raven went down to the lunchroom, which was full of families enjoying a Sunday brunch. She sat at a table, and while she looked over the menu, she noticed a pile of white sheets on the seat next to her. She realized all the families sitting around her—the mothers gently admonishing their children to sit up straight, wiping their chins, the fathers teasing their daughters—were Klan members.

Every time she told the story, she marveled at how normal people who loved each other and loved their children could engage in so much hate. Even now, in her eighties, she still couldn't fathom it. Raven believed there was no such thing as a small kindness, and she never hated anyone, even those who'd been so cruel to her. She embodied forgiveness to the very end. That night she was told to lock herself in her hotel room and not come out. For safety's sake. As night fell, she sat on her bed and saw through the window a fire burning in the distance. She got up to get a closer look and saw that it was no ordinary fire or festive bonfire. This was a cross burning on a hillside.

Heartbreakingly, Raven often had to leave the road early during such tours as things were simply getting too dangerous. But on one occasion, before she left the South, she had one final reminder, lest she question whether it was the right decision to return home. She was at the airport early one morning, dressed in an elegant circle skirt and dark glasses, à la Audrey Hepburn in *Roman Holiday*. She approached the counter of the coffee shop and asked for a cup of decaf with milk and sugar. The young waitress responded, "You'll have to go around back. We don't serve your kind here." Raven was livid. She knew segregation ruled the South, but this was an airport, federal property, subject to federal, not state law. This refusal of service was illegal. She stewed and pondered what to do, then decided the battle wasn't worth waging. Her peace of mind was worth more than tussling with a bigoted young woman over a cup of coffee. She turned and walked away to wait for her plane back to New York and back to her loving family.[3]

CHAPTER 6

DREAMS DEFERRED

I walked out of the doctor's office and into the bright glare of a June afternoon stunned and numb. Too numb to cry, in spite of the devastating news I'd just received. On June 17, 2012, two days after my New York debut as the Firebird, I withdrew from the remainder of the spring season because of my shin. An X-ray had revealed six stress fractures in my tibia. Three of them were "dreaded black-line fractures," meaning they were almost full breaks through the bone. The doctor, orthopedic surgeon to American Ballet Theatre and New York City Ballet, warned me that I might never dance again.

I knew the pain was like nothing I'd felt before, but I wasn't expecting this. Just days before, I had danced on the Met stage as the principal ballerina with ABT for a full house. Many of the attendees were people of color who were seeing themselves represented on that stage for the first time. It was an important step toward inclusion in classical ballet. More than a decade into my career, at last I could see what might be possible for me and generations of Black dancers to come. And now my career, my world, was crashing down around me.

I knew I had to keep moving forward and refused to accept his verdict. I had come too far to give up, however discouraged and terrified I felt. So I went for second, third, fourth, and fifth opinions, in search of a surgeon who believed they could put me back together again, though that was beginning to seem impossible.

I kept reminding myself of Raven's resolve—how she had quite literally risked her life to dance. Her ability to remain so passionate and committed to her art form, even when faced with unbelievable obstacles, was something I was in constant awe of; she proved again and again what it meant to persevere. And she probably would have continued with the Ballet Russe de Monte Carlo if her presence in the company hadn't also put everyone else in the company in danger of a violent attack by Southern segregationists. If Raven could overcome, I certainly could too—if I could just find the right medical team.

After months of research, I found one of the most qualified surgeons in New York City, Dr. Martin O'Malley, and we came up with a plan. His patients consisted of elite athletes from the NFL and the NBA, which put my mind at ease. Knowing that he had performed similar procedures on other elite "jumping" athletes many times before gave me hope. But this would be the first time he would be screwing a metal plate into the exterior of the tibia bone rather than the interior. A ballerina's "line" is vital to what she does, so one of his goals besides protecting and allowing a nearly broken bone to heal was to make sure my line still looked beautiful. Placed to the exterior, the plate was hidden between the tibia bone and the shin muscle in order to maintain the integrity of my line.

The surgery itself was a success, but I now faced a long road back to the stage. An unexpected consequence of the injury was that it gave me space to really pause for the first time since I had begun dancing sixteen years earlier. I was a woman now, and I could see more clearly than ever what I wanted, not only for myself but also for ballet. After meeting Raven, I now saw myself as part of a larger legacy of Black ballerinas, and it gave me a new perspective on ballet's history and the prospects for its future.

Though my dancing had been sidelined, I could still keep my promise to use my voice to tell Raven's story. So that's what I did. I shared just how important Raven was to me, and to ballet, at every opportunity and on every platform available to me. Meeting Raven had only underscored my mission: to be a champion for Black dancers, past and present. In addition to using traditional channels, I had started to embrace social media. I tried to use it in a way that allowed me to have honest conversations about race and my experiences in ballet, while spotlighting Black and brown dancers in the hopes of exposing a broader audience to the art form. And my greatest joy was having the ability and reach to raise awareness of the heroes and heroines who paved the way for me and others.

As the saying goes, when one door closes, another opens. Just before I had the surgery on my leg in the fall of 2012, a young editor from Simon & Schuster's Touchstone imprint reached out to me. She was interested in my writing a memoir. I remember thinking, "But I'm only in my twenties. I don't know that I have anything to say." Though I was hesitant, Gilda convinced me that my story, even just to this point, would help me continue to be an advocate for inclusion in ballet, even while having to spend time away from the stage due to injury.

Just as I was starting to lay the foundation for the memoir, which would come to be titled *Life in Motion*, another book opportunity presented itself. I was introduced to the brilliant illustrator and author Christopher Myers at G. P. Putnam's Sons Books for Young Readers, after hearing he was interested in working with me on an illustrated children's book.

That spring, as Christopher, our book editor, and I brainstormed ideas, Chris attended several of my performances. And after many conversations, we decided that the picture book we would create would be based on my relationship with Raven. That book became *Firebird*. Chris met Raven for the first time on a beautiful Sunday afternoon in July at Raven's and my favorite hangout spot, Café Luxembourg. He wanted to be around the two of us to get a true sense of our dynamic.

But first we had to get Raven through the restaurant entrance and the maze of tables to where Chris and I were seated. It was easier said than done because Raven knew everyone at Café Luxembourg, from the hostess to all of the waiters, and she greeted each of them affectionately as she made her way to us. Over mussels, french fries, and what had become Raven's favorite because it was mine, a glass of prosecco, Raven shared incredible stories from her life and career. Chris quickly fell under her spell. She spoke easily on a range of topics, from all she endured as a Black woman touring with the Ballet Russe in the Jim Crow South and having to leave her home country to continue her dance career in Amsterdam to the "good ol' days" of happily surviving on cigarettes and vodka while dancing in Europe.

It was one of those summer days that smells sweet and lives on in your memory. After several hours, I needed to go home and elevate my leg. I left Chris and Raven to continue their afternoon together. A day or so later, he shared his thoughts in an email, a true love letter to Raven:

> It was brilliant seeing your community of two in action, a gift to be sure. I love that she said she's up there with you onstage. I loved the way she danced in her chair while she told stories. I loved how full of stories she was. I also loved watching you with her, how much of

a gift you are to her and your generosity with that gift. The way you invite her to dream with you and invest in you. She is one of those folks with a prodigious gift for dreaming, and all she needs is a place to put it.

The afternoon had given him deep insight into the ballet sisterhood, and the eternal hold the art form has on the artist. Ballet, for those of us who love it, is not a career but a calling. In the email, he went on to describe how he could see that Raven had never stopped being a dancer, how she demonstrated learning to be a snowflake in *The Nutcracker*. At the table in Café Luxembourg, she had transformed herself back into a young ballerina with "fluttering hands" right before his eyes. They walked for hours after I left them, and on the way to Central Park, Raven pointed out the dance studio where she'd taken classes for years. Christopher felt she'd be ready to jump right in and take her place at the barre again. He'd delighted in our inside ballet jokes, Raven's laughing reminiscence about the time she "just *tendued* all the way across the stage." As I read Christopher's moving and eloquent account of the afternoon, I was thrilled that he'd been as captivated as I was by the magic of Raven. It didn't surprise me. Everyone who met her was immediately drawn to her warmth and joie de vivre. Christopher closed his email with the following:

Thanks for letting me in on Raven. She feels like such a good secret...even if everyone knows her, certainly that way she looks at you, like you were running some last miles in a marathon she started a long time ago, that was a gift for me to see.

The "last miles in a marathon she started a long time ago..." Chris had put it so perfectly and beautifully. I was in a "relay race," determined to complete it, not just for myself but for Raven, for all the Black ballerinas who had come before and for all the girls who would come after me. Giving up would not just mean defeat for me; it would mean thousands of dreams deferred all over again.

Still, rehab was a lonely experience. I felt a bit lost after such an incredibly successful and eventful 2012 spring season, the biggest of my career at ABT until that point. I certainly had my amazing support team, who called in to check on me around the clock, including, of course, Raven, who called at least once a week. I remember using those moments speaking with her to get some fresh air. I'd sit on the stoop of my Upper West Side apartment building, and I'd fill her in on every step of my recovery journey. She listened so patiently, wanting to hear every detail. She kept my spirits up with her infectious positive energy.

Raven was particularly intrigued by my discovery of Barre à Terre, "floor barre." This revolutionary exercise technique, created in the 1950s by Boris Kniaseff, involved me literally doing a ballet barre while lying on the floor of my living room. It had become a religion to me in my recovery. It was going to help me get back on my feet and finish the "last miles" of that marathon.

I explained the intricate yet simple exercises I was performing to keep up my technique. Raven found it so fascinating. But I also think her heartfelt interest was her clever way of distracting me by keeping our conversations light and positive. It was during those calls that my mind could take a break from the physical and mental stress, even if only for a brief moment.

November, the month after my surgery, was bleak. Raven continued making her weekly calls to check in on me and my recovery, but once in a while she'd sneak something in there about Olu. "How's Olu doing, Misty? Have you seen him lately? Has he come over to make you dinner?" she'd ask, half teasing. I could feel her smile through the phone when I told her he had.

Olu slowly came back into my life while I was recuperating. We had been apart for two years and had both grown so much. Olu never completely left in that time, but now he was right by my side, encouraging me and keeping me focused. He always believed I could accomplish anything I put my mind to and that recovering from this injury would be no different. Like Raven, Olu continued to maintain that I had a long career ahead and would dance all the ballets I dreamed of. Getting through this time brought us even closer, and though it went mostly unspoken, we were both aware that the door to romance was reopening.

I pushed through the pain of recovery, and though I had my incredible circle of support, I felt completely forgotten by ABT. The show must go on. The fall season had opened and closed without me, and two dancers who had joined the company a decade after me had been named principal dancers. Injured or not, that news hurt. My dreams felt further away than ever. I kept reminding myself, *Not just for you, but for Raven, too.*

By April 2013, only six months post-surgery, I returned to the stage in an intimate performance at the Brooklyn Academy of Music's black-box theater, dancing the iconic variation of the Dying Swan. I had *never* felt closer to the role. There was no need to look for my motivation: the Dying Swan was a metaphor for someone attempting to escape death, like I felt I just had as I recovered from a near career-ending injury.

But the most thrilling performance that spring took place on April 18, 2013, in the middle of my living room. Filmmaker Nelson George was moving forward with his idea for a documentary and came to film Raven and me for what would become *A Ballerina's Tale*. We spoke frequently over the phone, but I hadn't seen her in person in six months.

We had a small film crew recording us as we chatted and hung out. We were so comfortable with each other that we forgot we were on camera. Raven sat next to me, placing my surgery leg on her lap, examining it like it was the most beautiful sculpture she'd ever seen. She always brought light, love, and humor to every situation. She looked at the scar on my leg from where I had been cut open in surgery, a plate and several screws attached to my tibia to support the six stress fractures. She rubbed her fingers over my shin and said, "Oh, it looks beautiful; a good doctor is an artist.

I've bumped into my bed and my leg looked worse than that!" She went on to say how strong my ankles and feet were. All words of positivity and hope. Somehow, she always knew exactly what I needed to hear.

She marveled at the extent of my injury and how I continued to perform despite the pain. I had kept the enormity of what I was dealing with from almost everyone. But there are typical dance-related injuries and then there are the several fractures almost through the bone that I was dealing with, and I knew that both ABT and my close circle, Raven included, would have convinced me not to perform had they known the severity. And I would never have danced Firebird and proven to myself, ABT, and the ballet world that I could be the lead.

Raven and I must have sat in my living room for at least three hours that day talking about her life and career and what she thought of my career and ballet today. She said that seeing my performance of Firebird at the Met—and the audiences that attended—symbolized an era of change, and she was happy to have been there to witness it. She went on to note that she was excited not only for me but also for the younger dancers of color who were now in the company and that it gave her a sense of pride to observe the mentoring relationships I'd been developing with them.

The day of filming for the documentary ended with Raven and me linking hands and dancing the famous little swans variation from *Swan Lake*. We were completely in sync, as if we had danced this role together. Although generations apart, we spoke the same language. When Nelson and I looked at the footage, we knew the little swans moment was something special that had to be included in the film. This is a moment I hold so close to my heart, even today. We were bonded through roles we'd danced, through the ballet technique and language, and by being a part of the Black ballerina sisterhood.

A Ballerina's Tale made its world premiere at Tribeca Film Festival, and Raven was the star. We made sure she was there in all her glory to be celebrated by an at-capacity theater. The audience roared with laughter and applause in response to her scene. It was an incredible feeling to share the red carpet, and the screen, with Raven. Afterward, during the Q and A, Nelson acknowledged Raven from the stage: "One of the most amazing people in the film is here tonight, and I just want to give her a special shout-out because she's so wonderful, and that is Raven Wilkinson." Raven stood up to thunderous applause. Finally, she was receiving her due as an artist and a pioneer.

I made it through my first season back onstage in 2013. I wrote in my journal:

May 13

Dryad Queen in *Don Quixote* will be my only debut this season. Everything else I've danced before. I will dance Gulnare in *Le Corsaire*, Pas de Trois in *Swan Lake*, the lead harlot in *Romeo and Juliet*, a fairy in *Sleeping*

Beauty, as well as Princess Florine. I'm really just happy to be mentally ready to be back onstage and to have an opportunity to at least attempt Dryad Queen. Still getting there physically.

May 28

Tonight was my second show back at the Met since my procedure and second performance as Dryad Queen. I'm so glad that I proved to myself that I was capable. The variation was easy, and I felt very relaxed. What a wonderful feeling to be back.

My body was still catching up to what my brain knew I was capable of doing, and I needed Kevin to believe I would get there again. I was committed to taking a more proactive role in my own career and hoped to get more experience in principal roles. I even went so far as to reach out to the director of the Royal Ballet in London after their superstar, Steven McRae, made his ABT debut as Lankendem alongside me as Gulnare in *Le Corsaire.*

Steven and I had formed a great partnership. His director flew in to see our show and was extremely complimentary. Steven and I proposed that I join him at the Royal Ballet as a guest artist in *Romeo and Juliet.* I felt this could be a real opportunity as well as the nudge Kevin needed to see me in a new light. But the invitation never came.

Although my recovery was gaining momentum, I felt as though I'd had the rug pulled out from under me when I learned that I would not be performing the role of Gulnare on our tour to my hometown of Los Angeles. It was a dagger to my heart because it was a role I had danced for the last four years. But Kevin explained to me that though I had just performed the role during our season at the Met, the casting for the Music Center had been made months before the season started, unbeknownst to me. With my physical uncertainty post-surgery, he couldn't commit to casting me in the role of Gulnare so far in advance. It was difficult to hear but a part of the inner workings of dancing with a company. Once again I tried not to let this setback crush my faith and destroy my dream. But it was hard not to imagine the worst: I would be yet another Black ballerina whose career did not reach its full potential.

Driven off the Stage

As the fifties were drawing to a close, Raven was being celebrated for her talent as a dancer. The Chicago papers, in particular, consistently praised her work. In one review, dance critic
Ann Barzel called her "Outstanding... Raven Wilkinson of the
beautiful feet." In another, Barzel mentioned her and Eleanor
among "Girls who consistently have impressed us." A December
1959 review by the same critic said, "Several noteworthy performances were applauded during the evening. Raven Wilkinson
danced a beautiful lyric waltz in *Les Sylphides*."[1] And last but not
least, another Chicago critic, Louis Guzzo, credited Raven and
several other Ballet Russe dancers with raising the bar for the
entire company, writing, "The difference was notable with the
first appearance of the ensemble in *Les Sylphides*. The other principals, Irina Borowska, Tatiana Grantzeva, and Raven Wilkinson also reflected the new order of things."[2]

Beautiful feet, lyricism, "principal." No one mentioned or

seemed to notice Raven's race. That was not the situation in the South. Corps de ballet member Margery Beddow recalled a harrowing trip below the Mason-Dixon Line: "Riding through the countryside, we suddenly noticed in the distance a cross burning on the side of a hill. As we drew nearer, we could make out the white figures of the Ku Klux Klan. They were making a human barricade across the highway and stopping and searching every car, truck, and bus. Our stage manager, Lou Smith, stood up in the bus and, turning to us, said, 'Everyone stay in your assigned seat and hold on tight. We're not stopping. We're going through.' You could feel the tension snap into the air. Well, we got that old bus up to about eighty miles an hour, and at the last possible moment the Klansmen jumped out of the way. We all looked at Wilkinson and breathed a communal sigh of relief."[3]

Other episodes didn't end so smoothly. One of the more terrifying moments Raven shared was yet another visit to Montgomery, Alabama. Klansmen showed up at the theater during rehearsals. To everyone's complete shock, they stormed onto the stage. The male dancers instinctively stood in front of Raven. The entire company froze in place. One of the Klansmen bellowed: "Which one of you is the nigger?"

No one answered. They just stood there, motionless and without reacting. Their physical discipline and stage training came in handy in this dangerous moment. Frustrated, the Klansmen went from dancer to dancer, staring them down and demanding to know "Are you the nigger?" "Are you?" They were confused because several of the dancers had darker complexions.

Finally, the police showed up, having been called by the stage manager, and chased the Klansmen away. But the stakes were crystal clear: Raven couldn't afford to just brush off the incident and dance onstage that night. The Klan didn't simply want to intimidate her. If given the chance, they would kill her. As would often happen in such cases, Raven was sent back to New York and invited to rejoin the tour once the company had left the South.

It had reached the point where she could no longer tour in the South at all. It was too dangerous for her and for the rest of the company. One of her staunchest supporters in these life-threatening moments was principal dancer and, eventually, company leader, Nina Novak. "These people are very ignorant," she would commiserate, and then she would share her parallel experiences with Nazis in her native Poland during the Second World War.[4]

So Raven was quite shocked when on a bus trip to an engagement in Philadelphia, Nina turned to her and said, "You've really gone as far as you can with this company. You could never be a white swan." Raven was flabbergasted. Nina and Alicia Alonso had considered not dancing in protest after the "Which one of you is the nigger" incident. Now, here Nina was setting a permanent glass ceiling on Raven's aspirations.

Nina had always been demanding, and sometimes even sharp, in her remarks. During a summer season at Wollman Rink, right in the heart of New York's Central Park, Raven, who was always upbeat, was laughing with other dancers. Nina snapped, "If you laugh so much, I don't think you're serious." But Raven had respected Nina's courage as an artist who took chances and valued her emotional support in those terrifying episodes.[5]

Raven thought Nina saw her as "just a human being and artist." But then Nina continued with a condescending statement that made it clear she didn't "see" Raven at all: "Maybe you should go and start your own company. An African dance troupe." Raven was stunned and seethed inside. She'd devoted her life to ballet. She had every respect for African culture, but like all serious ballet dancers of the period, she'd only ever really been trained in that one dance form. Nina's comment felt like all those years of dedication hadn't been noticed at all. They saw only her color. Raven felt reduced to a stereotype.

Eleanor D'Antuono believed that Nina was somewhat envious of Raven and trying to put her in her place.[6] When Raven would tell the story, it was clear the insult still stung decades later. And yet she could still manage to be forgiving, saying, "Life is a patchwork. People are a patchwork."[7] In spite of Nina Novak's insult, which Raven never forgot, she could still remember the good she had done.

The company was beginning to lose some of its luster, and

Mr. Denham began to give more and more control to Novak. Eleanor felt it was time to leave. Raven agreed: "When I left the Ballet Russe, it was time for me to go. Union problems, salary problems."[8] She was also exhausted by the pressures of having to leave every time they headed South and rejoin when they were in "safe" territory. The conversation with Nina on the way to Philadelphia had been the last straw. It was bad enough to have her life threatened by white supremacists, but to be insulted to her face by someone she considered a colleague, a friend, and a peer was an affront she couldn't overcome. She also wanted to leave before the racial situation deteriorated to the point that they had to let her go.[9]

When she went to see Mr. Denham to announce her decision, he claimed she had never told him what she was experiencing in the South. Raven found this impossible to believe. I understood Raven's surprise. I have experienced a similar lack of empathy and recognition of racial circumstances from my white colleagues throughout my career. In May 2007, when the *New York Times* printed a feature titled "Where Are All the Black Swans?" which shone a spotlight on the ballet community, none of my colleagues at ABT understood why I was upset by the harsh truth that the article highlighted. It criticized the ballet world and named major ballet companies, including ABT, for their lack of career possibilities for Black women historically in classical ballet. I remember trying to have conversations that day with some of my colleagues, and rather than compassion and understanding from them, there were skeptical questions about why I felt the way I did.

Many Black dancers in major companies still feel that way today when our colleagues are surprised at the violence and discrimination we continue to experience. When we shared our true stories during the racial reckoning of the summer of 2020 within our companies and across organizations, they were usually met with shock and murmurs of "I had no idea." This has been the source of so many enduring problems: the two Americas, and the unawareness of a large segment of the population who've lived a different history. Fortunately, an honest dialogue has finally begun, from boardrooms to ballet studios.

Raven began that conversation with the most prestigious American company of its time almost seventy years ago. Not only was she an exquisite ballerina, but she was also a champion for truth and equality.

But the day Raven had her heart-to-heart with Mr. Denham, he stood firm in his denial. Then he went on the attack, saying to Raven, "After all I have done for you, that you would do this to me. I took you into this company even though you are Black." He'd hit a raw nerve.

Raven stood up to the full height of her five feet, two inches and shot back:

"I am an American and you should know as a foreigner, that is completely irresponsible for you to say."[10] This was a rare moment when the usually gentle and patient Raven was completely and understandably furious. She no doubt felt like her mother did, and like so many Black Americans do, when our right to be in a space is questioned. We who have been here for four hundred years, we who have built the country, fought and died for it, are continuously asked to prove our worthiness for citizenship. Raven had risked her life and swallowed her pride to dance, to bring honor to the company. Now its leader, a Russian émigré, was telling her she owed him a debt for giving her an opportunity she'd earned.

As an older woman, Raven grew philosophical about the incident. "When I look back, I had no business being so angry... I can afford to say he did do something he didn't have to do and that very few have done since."[11] Denham did the right thing, but it's impossible to know if it was entirely altruistic, as he also enjoyed showing Raven off to donors and important backstage visitors. Even when she was just a corps de ballet member, he would single her out to introduce her, like a curiosity.[12]

Looking back at all that Raven tolerated, with so much patience and grace, I feel for her. Following her departure from Ballet Russe, Raven went from company to company and auditioned: New York City Ballet, ABT, Pennsylvania Ballet. None would take her. In 1960, at age twenty-six, her career appeared to be all but finished.

The Klan had driven her off the stages of Montgomery, Birmingham, and Atlanta. And the prejudice and lack of opportunity for people of color that permeated the ballet world wore her down in her own country. After leaving the Ballet Russe de Monte Carlo, the woman who'd received so many reviews calling her a standout, graceful, a principal…never danced for an American ballet company again.

In hindsight, I can't help but wonder what might have been.

CHAPTER 7

BLACK SWANS ROCK

The 2013 Los Angeles summer season came and went. I put my head down and continued working hard to reach an even more evolved place physically and artistically in my dancing than I had been pre-injury. I was still working privately with my floor barre teacher to strengthen my body and finesse my technique as well as taking Pilates and Gyrotonic classes. If I wasn't onstage performing with ABT, I was in the studio working on my own. I would rent studio space at Steps on Broadway on West Seventy-Fourth Street in the heart of the Upper West Side. I'd walk up the steep four flights of narrow stairs, and in a mirrored studio, I'd work on different lead variations just to challenge myself. It's not uncommon for dancers to push themselves outside the confines of their companies. More opportunity can often come if the artistic staff sees growth, particularly coming out of an "off" season. This was something I always felt I needed to do to give myself some control over my career.

Following the tour, Kevin and I spoke about what the next season would look like for me. He mentioned the possibility of my dancing more principal roles in the near future, including Cinderella, and Swanilda in *Coppélia*, the ballet about a doll who comes to life that had enchanted Raven as a child and first sparked her interest in the art form. What budding "Ravens" could I inspire if given the opportunity to dance those iconic fairy-tale roles? But those factors never entered into the artistic leadership's thinking, and Kevin's vague promises didn't reassure me. After so many years in the company, I knew not to get my hopes up. The company's actions spoke louder than his words.

In October, another promotion of a dancer who'd been with the company for only a handful of years was announced, reminding me of my own uncertain future. I was in year twelve with the company, year six as a soloist. Most of those who were in the corps or remained at the soloist level that long had little to no chance of going further. It usually meant that Kevin had made up his mind about them. I was concerned that Kevin had made up his mind about me.

Though I felt discouraged, I no longer felt powerless or alone. I knew the value I brought to the company, both through my dancing and through my ability to increase and diversify the audience. People who had once felt apprehensive entering a space like the Metropolitan Opera House and people who'd never seen a ballet before were coming to my performances. And while overcoming a career-threatening injury had shown me what I was made of, my expanding repertoire was showing me what I was capable of if given the chance. As usual, I turned to Raven for advice. And once again, she advised me to speak to Kevin about my concerns. From Raven's perspective, honest communication was the only way forward. When I spoke with Olu, his counsel was the same. Without hesitation, I followed their advice.

On October 4, I made my way to Kevin's office through the maze of cubbies and wooden desks that have lined the floors of ABT's administrative offices since the 1980s. I sat across from him, surrounded by posters of dancers from seasons past: Alessandra Ferri, Julio Bocca, Julie Kent. As much as I identified with this community of committed ballet dancers, even the signage around ABT reminded me of my solitude as the lone Black woman at my level.

I spoke with confidence and conviction.

"Kevin," I began, "I want to speak with you before another season, another year, goes by."

"I'm so happy you are here," he responded. "You have been on my mind, and I've been meaning to talk to you about the level of your focus, commitment, and the growth I'm seeing in your dancing." I was shocked. Kevin had never spoken so directly to me before. Most artistic meetings were so cryptic that you walked out still uncertain about where you stood, replaying what was said in your mind, attempting to decode the meaning. But here Kevin was, happy to see me and eager to talk.

We had a wide-ranging discussion on all that I had been experiencing since the injury. The relationship between artistic director and dancer is a complicated one. Kevin had known me since I was sixteen and in the studio company, and it can often be difficult for both parties to see the growth and evolution of the other. We discussed a range of topics from the studio to the stage and beyond, even touching on race, one of the most taboo subjects of all. It was the first time I felt like he was seeing me as the full woman I was.

Kevin admitted that from *day one*, he'd hoped that I understood and could carry the responsibility and weight of being a Black woman in this art form. After thirteen years at ABT, I certainly did. I lived it every day. But this was progress and was the first time he'd articulated how much he thought about the historic meaning of my career.

He then acknowledged my development and maturity as an artist and a representative of both ABT and ballet, but that the timing of my injuries had slowed my ascension within the company. I took a deep breath, prepared to have my expectations managed, to be told to be patient and wait my turn. Instead, he continued:

"I'd like to prepare you for *Swan Lake* this year. I'm kicking myself for not preparing you last year, when we had to bring in a guest artist because of injuries."

He continued. "We're going to be celebrating ABT's seventy-fifth anniversary in the 2014–2015 season. This is going to be a monumental year for you personally and for the company," Kevin shared. "I have a plan for you, but I need to hear you say that you're comfortable enough in your skin and as an artist to take ownership of these principal roles. Because they're coming."

"I'm ready, Kevin," I answered before he could fully get the words out.

I walked out of his office in a daze. I was to prepare for Odette/Odile, not a cygnet, not the pas de trois, but *the Swan Queen*. On my way through the hallways, I passed one of the posters for *Swan Lake*, a beautiful photograph of the Swan Queen emerging from a real lake to embrace her Prince Siegfried, her true love. I was going to be that queen, from taking my first ballet class on a basketball court at thirteen years old to now, performing the most iconic role in the entire ballet canon. I was so ready to get to work.

I thought of Raven in a group shot from the Ballet Russe de Monte Carlo, in her black leotard and pale tights, sitting *next to* a white ballerina dressed as the Swan Queen. The look in Raven's eyes felt familiar, as if she were asking, "Do you see me? Really see me?" I couldn't wait to call and tell her, "Yes, they see *us*!"

When we spoke that evening, she confessed that though she was confident after watching me in *Firebird* that I could take on Odette/Odile, if she was being honest, she wasn't quite sure it would ever happen. "But I should have had faith," she added joyfully.

Later that month, I was honored by Black Girls Rock! with the Young, Gifted & Black Award. BGR was a nationally televised event sponsored by Black Entertainment Television. It's a huge celebration of Black women who break boundaries, blaze trails, and set trends across a variety of fields. That night I was to be honored alongside Queen Latifah, Venus Williams, Marian Wright Edelman, and Ameena Matthews, and I performed with fellow honoree Patti LaBelle. Gilda and I made sure Raven was there, in a box seat stage right, to share in this celebration. Though the wider audience was unaware, that night was an opportunity for Raven and me to celebrate what felt like a new chapter for me at ABT and for ballet in general.

It is not common that a ballerina is celebrated on a national awards show, and certainly not common to be featured in a performance alongside a legend like Patti LaBelle, but I opened her performance with a solo before she took the stage singing her hit song "You Are My Friend." The beauty of what the Black Girls Rock! Awards and BET showed on the screen during our performance was not just the balletic movements of my arms and body but also the specific close-up shots of my feet, wearing brown—not pink—pointe shoes. It may seem minor, but it was, in fact, an important and meaningful detail. For Black ballerinas, our daily regimen includes having to dye the pink satin the shoes come in, to bring the color closer to the brown-hued tones of our skin. Dance Theatre of Harlem was at the forefront of this movement throughout its history and now this important and necessary part of our experience as Black and brown women in ballet was televised around the world.

Although the performance was certainly a highlight of the night for me, the pinnacle was when I took the stage to accept my award and I was able, for the first time, to thank Raven in front of a national audience. I looked at her as I began my acceptance speech:

I step back and look at my life, and more often than not I wonder who and where I would be without ballet. As one of six kids growing up in a single-parent home struggling to get by, I found my voice through dance. For over a decade, I was the only Black woman in my company. Today I am proud to see young, talented ballerinas like Erica Lall, who confidently says her goal is to one day climb the heights of ballet to become a principal dancer. That's when I am reminded of my purpose, to be for them what I didn't have as a young ballerina—a mentor, a role model, someone who looks like them.

I have to thank Beverly Bond and the Black Girls Rock! organization for this honor tonight and your amazing girls for opening your doors to me. Thank you to Debra Lee and BET for acknowledging my achievements and for honoring ballet at this level.

Thank you to my family, and to my ballet teacher Cynthia Bradley, who discovered me at age thirteen on a basketball court of the Boys and Girls Club. The legendary ballerina Raven Wilkinson, who is here with me tonight and is SUCH an inspiration, and every Black ballerina who has paved the way for me to dance. I'd also like to thank American Ballet Theatre for giving me a platform and continuing to let my voice be heard.

And last but not least, my incredible fans, who show me so much love and support and help remind me that what I stand for is important and so much bigger than me! You keep me pushing through on the toughest of days and when I feel alone. I now know I'm not alone because you all stand behind me, in every rehearsal and on every stage.

Black girls DO Rock.

Black girls CAN be ballerinas.

It was a big night for me and for everyone who'd been on the journey with me. After the show ended, I had a chance to take a breath and absorb the moment. My guests and I gathered in my dressing room backstage. Raven looked beautiful, wearing a red, purple, and gold tapestry jacket and black pants with her hair in a modest bun. She glowed with excitement as we digested the evening. "Oh, Misty, you danced so beautifully up there! And you gave Patti LaBelle an appropriately grand introduction to the stage," she gushed. "What a treat it was to see ballet performed as part of *this* show! And your speech was so wonderful! Think of how many little brown girls will get to see all of this! I'm so proud of you!"

Raven really had a way of making everyone around her feel special. And on that night, I was the lucky recipient. Before we left the dressing room to go to the after-party, where Raven mingled, drank, and danced into the night, we took a photo, posed cheek to cheek with smiles bigger than us, that I still hold close to my heart. It was an incredible night and one that I felt so blessed to share with Raven, my hero.

CHAPTER 8

BLOOD, SWEAT, AND
SWAN QUEENS

One of the privileges of dancing with an international ballet company is the opportunity to tour and travel the world. But that privilege comes at a price. When I landed in Brisbane, Australia, on August 26, 2014, for my *Swan Lake* debut, my body felt as though I'd made the twenty-three-hour-and-forty-eight-minute journey hopping from one foot to the other in "emboîté," like the line of "little swans" in their entrance. Every bone and muscle felt wrecked. But exhausted or not, the very next morning, I had to be ready to report to the Queensland Performing Arts Center's Lyric Theater for the all-important technical rehearsal.

That night, I slept only a couple of hours in anticipation of the day ahead. Feeling antsy, I got up and made myself a bowl of oatmeal, something that was familiar and comforting. I packed my dance bag with newly sewn pointe shoes and snacks for the day and made my way to the theater. The weather was absolute perfection this time of year, a sunny seventy-eight degrees, and as I walked to the Arts Center, I couldn't help but feel calmed seeing the Brisbane River, which runs along the theater. It felt almost like I was back in my native California with the dry, warm climate and soothing breezes.

The Queensland Performing Arts Center was an impressive sight to behold from across the river. The white modernist structure shone like a welcoming beacon, bathed in festive light. For a moment during that walk I was at peace. But as I approached the stage door, uneasiness over the task at hand came back, and I had to remind myself, "This is just another tech rehearsal. You've been doing this for almost half your life. You got this." As much as I tried to convince myself that this was an ordinary day in order to stay grounded, it wasn't. I was only hours away from the technical rehearsal for my historic debut as the Swan Queen in *Swan Lake.*

Just inside the stage door was a tunnel that led straight to the backstage and dressing rooms. I picked up my overstuffed theater case from the rack on my way to the room I shared with three other soloists. It was a typical guest performer's dressing room: small and sterile, white walls lined with mirrors and lights with rolling hanging racks for our costumes. I opened my case, filled with tights, leotards, and warm-ups. At the bottom, buried beneath all the clothes, was a large manila envelope, old and falling apart. I keep it filled to the max with pictures and personal cards and notes from the time I joined ABT until the present. I dug through the envelope as I do at every theater where we perform and picked out the exact images and cards I needed for this moment. I taped pictures of my nieces and nephews (my two sisters' and eldest brother's children), of some of my closest friends, of Olu and me, and of course of me and Raven, to the mirror. The one Raven and I had taken at Black Girls Rock!, cheek to cheek, beaming from that magical night. I needed them all close to help make the dressing room feel like I had a piece of home with me.

I told myself I was ready to take on this day. Even though my big rehearsal in the theater took place only a day after I landed in Australia, I had some peace of mind knowing that I had two weeks for my body to adjust to the time change before my debut as Odette/Odile, *the* Swan Queen in *Swan Lake*, the ultimate classical role, in the ultimate classical ballet. But I had to pull it together for this tech rehearsal, which, like a performance, is done with lights, costume, makeup, and full orchestra. But something was off that day, and I was beginning to feel removed from my body. During the many months of preparation in the studio, I hadn't ever felt this kind of unease. But today I felt unsure and off-kilter. Now that I was here in Brisbane and in the theater, it all suddenly became very real. I was feeling the pressure.

I kept reminding myself of what Raven said to me when I told her I'd be dancing Odette/Odile: "After seeing you as the Firebird, I knew that Swan Queen was ideal for you because of your freedom and creature-like use of your back and arms, which are truly unique." Her words were the Holy Grail to me.

Yet doubt kept creeping in.

Performing as the Firebird was different, and my version was a modern take on a classic that had been created for me with all my best attributes considered by the choreographer, Alexei Ratmansky. The Firebird character is wild and free; she is not in a romantic relationship with the male lead, but a spiritual, independent force of fire and strength. This is within the realm of what Black dancers "can do." Or at least, that's what we're told, and on some level that's what I had always believed.

Throughout history, Black dancers haven't been given opportunities to be seen as romantic leads, layered in character, soft and elusive. The Swan Queen's character was vastly different from the Firebird's. She is the ultimate embodiment of feminine grace, purity, and love. A princess turned into a swan by an evil sorcerer, Von Rothbart, she is doomed to live by a lake with other white swans until a prince vows true love. Prince Siegfried meets her on his twenty-first birthday, while out hunting, falls in love at first sight, and vows to deliver her from her curse. At his birthday ball that evening, Von Rothbart arrives in disguise with a beautiful black swan, Odile, who beguiles the prince into breaking his vow, thereby condemning Odette to remain a swan forever.

Dancing the dual role of Odette/Odile wouldn't be just a physical feat; it would mean the undoing of a lot of emotional and psychological trauma. Black ballerina generational trauma I carried with me. It was embedded into the very fabric of ballet, and specifically *Swan Lake*, one of the most famous of the ballets blancs—or white ballets—as they are called. Black women throughout history are not typically cast in *Swan Lake* for fear of ruining the visual continuity of white bodies on the stage. Other than Houston Ballet's Lauren Anderson, no Black woman had performed the full-length *Swan Lake* in a major company before me, and certainly not with ABT.

When I learned I would be taking on this role, I was thrilled but completely shocked and overwhelmed. *Swan Lake* was the first ballet I performed with ABT on the stage of the Metropolitan Opera House when I was nineteen years old. I was a brand-new company member in my first spring season, and I was cast to perform a swan in the corps de ballet. I was told to dust my skin with white foundation and powder to fit in with the white dancers, a common practice in classical companies for the few Black dancers in the ballet blanc repertoire. So I never once allowed myself to dream of dancing the lead.

As time pressed on throughout rehearsals and coaching sessions to prepare for the role over several months, I toggled between feeling ready to take on the role and wondering if I could really rise to the occasion amid not just the doubts and pressures of the ballet community, but more importantly, my own. *Of all the Black ballerinas who've worked and dreamed and never got this chance, why should it be me? I've wanted the opportunity, and I know I worked hard to earn it, but can I pull this off? Am I truly worthy?* I agonized.

These crippling doubts battled with Raven's motivation as I readied for the tech rehearsal. I slipped into the chiffon nightgown that the princess who becomes the Swan Queen wears in the prologue as she wanders through the forest and is captured by the evil sorcerer, Von Rothbart. I headed to the hair and makeup room, as I still had no idea how I would style my curly hair to appear tame and silky as the princess. Reva, the principal hair and makeup artist, looked at my hair and said in her thick Russian accent, "Do you just want to wear a half wig?" I didn't realize I needed such preparations. We typically only get about thirty minutes to do hair and makeup for a tech rehearsal, in between class and spacing rehearsals, and I would need more time to get my hair situated. So I told Reva, "For this tech, I'll stick with my natural hair." I needed to use the time to gather my thoughts and emotions and focus on my dancing more than I needed silky hair for a rehearsal.

The rehearsal began, and I made my quick entrance as the princess and returned to hair and makeup to transform into Odette. Then I stood in the wings with the corps and the solo swans all around me preparing to take the stage for the first time as the Swan Queen. The music started to build before my entrance, and I quite literally began to panic. As the music played, and the notes sounded, my mind and body drifted out of sync. It was as though I were nineteen years old again, in the corps de ballet, preparing to dance *Swan Lake* for the very first time. I felt like an impostor, an intruder. Who did I think I was, standing in the wings about to jeté onto the stage as the Swan Queen? My body was rejecting being the lead.

The string section built to a crescendo, and I leapt out onto the stage, landing in the ballet's first iconic swan pose. My heart was pounding. I stepped into the first of several piqué arabesques, and the rest was a blur. I went through the motions and got through the pantomime sequence where the Swan Queen tells Prince Siegfried the story of how she was captured by an evil sorcerer and turned into a swan and only a vow of true love can break the spell and return her to human form. *My* internal evil sorcerer was the nagging doubt *"Can I be the ballerina?"*

I exited the stage in a bit of a trance. I sat in the wings feeling lost as I watched the twenty-four swans—the corps dancers— take the stage. *That's where you belong,* my mind was telling me. *Who are you to be the Swan Queen?* I tried to internalize Raven's mantra, "I come here as an artist and a human being." But in that moment, I could only focus on the fact that I was *the first Black woman at ABT* to dance this role. And if I failed, I would probably be the last. That's how fragile opportunities often are for people of color. Your failures close the door for anyone aspiring to follow in your footsteps.

I attempted to push those thoughts out. I entered the stage again and began the pas de deux with the prince, but I was hearing the exquisite music through the ears of my nineteen-year-old self, the ears of a corps dancer. *You should be dancing on the side with them, in a long line, not center stage, being lifted to the sky by a prince.* It was as if the notes that Odette dances to, the mournful violin solo, weren't there. I could only hear the corps music cues.

Somehow, I made it through the confusing out-of-body experience of this rehearsal. The artistic staff had a ton of notes, as they often do, but the feedback I received was nowhere near as bad as I felt. They mostly addressed staging concerns, like finding my marks, which wings I would enter and exit out of, and timing for musical cues with the conductor. While they were focused on technical issues, I was focused on not disappointing every Black dancer who came before me or ruining the chances of those who might come after me. I still had two full weeks to take it all in before I had to face down my own evil sorcerer in the actual performance.

I had thrown myself into preparing for this day eleven months before, in October 2013, when Kevin told me I would learn the role. He had me begin with the second-act entrance and pas de deux, just to be ready in the event that I would be cast or put on at the last minute if there were any injuries. I immediately started the process of learning what Kevin and ballet mistress Irina Kolpakova had shown me to be the basic vocabulary of the Swan Queen. The Swan Queen's language is verbalized through her arms and back, which, when properly used, become a set of wings.

The first thing I learned was the pantomime sequence from Odette's first entrance in the second act and the first time she comes face-to-face with Prince Siegfried. Siegfried has just left his twenty-first birthday celebration with his mother's gift of a crossbow in hand. Overwhelmed by the pressure to find a bride, as he is to become king, he seeks solace in the woods, when he comes upon a magnificent swan in flight. He begins to take aim, but to his surprise she transforms into a beautiful girl right before his eyes. He retreats to observe her, but out of curiosity he steps out only to startle her. He assures her he will do her no harm and asks her to explain the wonder he has just seen. So she tells him the story of how she became a swan. Kevin taught me this sequence, actually speaking words to the mime phrases in time with the music, like a lullaby, as he demonstrated it.

The prince grabs hold of her hand to calm her down and asks her who she is. "I am the Queen of the Swans," she says, and he bows to her. She is surprised that he would treat her with such reverence. She responds by motioning for him to come with her as she leads him to the lake. "Over there is the lake of my mother's tears." She then points toward the evil sorcerer's lair. "And over there is one strong man who took my heart and broke it." The prince attempts to speak, but she stops him: "But wait, if one swears eternal love to me, I will be a swan no more." To this day I sing those phrases in my head as I'm performing this section. And though this sequence is pantomime and not dancing, it's the foundation for Odette's character and the *Swan Lake* story.

After all the months of preparation and anticipation, here I was, in Brisbane, Australia, about to debut the role in front of an audience of two thousand people. Despite all the work I'd put into transforming myself into the Swan Queen, I needed Raven's determination and faith more than ever.

We didn't speak while I was in Australia. Raven could be hard to get in touch with, even when we were in the same time zone. She didn't own a cell phone, nor did she have call-waiting on her home phone, so I often got a busy signal when I'd try her. Still, I felt Raven was 100 percent with me. The thing about Raven was that when she spoke, her words had great impact on me, so if she told me, as she did when we spoke every day leading up to my departure, that I was ready, then I was ready. I just had to believe it myself.

I woke up the morning of the show and finally felt at peace. As nervous as I had been and as badly as that tech rehearsal had gone, I was now able to accept that I was completely prepared. And Raven's words rang louder than ever in my mind. Everything was falling into place.

On September 3, I arrived at the theater early, as I typically do on performance day. I had made the decision to prep my hair by blowing it out and curling it to get a good base so that I could wear it down in the opening scene, eschewing Reva's offer of a wig. I pinned my hair in a loose low bun and headed to company class to warm up. I broke in a new pair of pointe shoes so that I would have a harder pair to add to the pile of shoes I had picked out for different sections of the ballet. All were labeled in ink on the bottom: "Second-act entrance and pas de deux" (strong shoes to keep me supported through the long, partnered section), "Second-act variation" (a good balance of supple and strong for a combination of jumps and pirouettes), "Third-act pas de deux" (strong for when I'm Odile, the black swan, tackling technically precise footwork), and "Third-act variation and coda" (for all those fouettés). I would reuse a pair from the third-act pas de deux for the fourth act. Yes, I wore four pairs of pointe shoes in my first *Swan Lake* with ABT. It was pretty ridiculous and definitely a sign of how nervous I was. I would never do that again any other time I danced this role.

After class I headed to hair and makeup, where my hair was pulled into a half-up, half-down do for my entrance in the first act as a young, innocent princess. Back in the small dressing room, I sat surrounded by flowers and cards with well-wishes from company members and staff as I worked to focus my mind. I stared long and hard at the photograph of Raven and me. This was *our* moment.

At the half-hour call, wearing the princess gown, my

full-length leg warmers that cover me from hip to heel and a sleeveless vest to keep my back warm, I went to get acquainted with the stage—to feel the floor and energy before the curtain went up. I could hear Raven's soft but insistent tones: "I'll be the wind at your back." Irina and Kevin each spent some one-on-one time with me, letting me know how proud they were and how ready I was to take this on. I couldn't help but wonder if this opportunity would be happening at all if Raven hadn't emboldened me to have that meeting with Kevin. But now wasn't the time to wonder. I had to stay centered.

Moments later, I stood stage right in a pool of blue light, waiting for the stage manager to give me my cue to enter. I was calm and at ease, completely in my body. I let the exquisite notes of the Tchaikovsky score fill my spirit. I ran out onto the stage, and the audience erupted into applause. Raven's positive encouragement and energy followed me to the stage, and I felt right at home.

After my first entrance, my dresser took me by the hand and ran me back to hair and makeup, where my hair was pulled into a low bun and my body was covered in brown powder to take away the shine on my skin, so I looked less human as I transformed from a princess to a swan. I'm proud to say that I was no longer adhering to covering my body in white makeup, as I had when I was in the corps de ballet. The second act felt exactly how I dreamed it would. I heard every single note of Odette's music during the pas de deux. I connected with my partner,

Alex Hammoudi, as we fell in love on the stage as Odette and Prince Siegfried.

By the time the third act came around, my body was extremely warm, and my surgery leg felt ready to take on the technical challenges. During the "Great Hall" scene, where the prince is to choose his bride, I performed the demanding thirty-two fouettés, the big tour de force everyone looks for from the evil swan, Odile, with no problem. This is one of the most technically challenging parts in the ballet. I savored every moment of the final act, when the heartbroken prince comes to beg for Odette's forgiveness for breaking his vow of eternal love and betraying her with the evil black swan, Odile. I let the music transport me, right up to the cliff above the lake from which I leapt, to my death, followed by the prince, who couldn't bear to live without me. Moments later, Alex and I stood on the platform, appearing to the audience to be ascending in a radiant cloud, two lovers reunited in the afterlife. And I was on cloud nine. WE HAD DONE IT! I, a Black ballerina, had "touched the sky."

Days later, I returned home to New York. One of my first calls was to Raven. We talked for hours. A friend of hers had shown her a clip from my performance that had been posted on the Queensland Performing Arts Center website immediately following my show. The first thing Raven commented on were my fouettés in the third act. This shocked me and made me a bit nervous. That was the part of the performance I was least confident about. It's the one part of the ballet where I often felt removed and out of character. But Raven assured me, "I saw your artistry in those turns." I had received flowers, cards, and congratulations from Kevin, from Irina, from fans I'd never met, all of which I truly appreciated. Yet it was Raven's words that made me feel I'd overcome a huge hurdle. At least for those two weeks in Australia, I had conquered my doubts.

Most importantly, I was humbled that my performance answered the questions Raven had asked in an interview with *Pointe* magazine: "When are we going to get a Swan Queen of a darker hue? How long can we deny people that position? Do we feel aesthetically we can't face it? I think until we start seeing it regularly, we'll never believe it. But I'm sure that it won't take another sixty years to happen."[1]

It didn't take another sixty years. In fact, it had happened within a year of Raven speaking those words. And soon I would be asked to dance the role on the greatest stage of all: the Metropolitan Opera House.

CHAPTER 9

LIVE BY THE SWAN, DIE BY THE SWAN

When 2015 began, I viewed it as a year of infinite possibilities. That spring's Met season, my fourteenth and ABT's seventy-fifth, would be the most challenging but most fulfilling of my career. Throughout those eight weeks, I would be making principal debuts as the Cowgirl in Agnes de Mille's *Rodeo*, the waltz solo from *Les Sylphides*, which was Raven's signature role, Juliet in *Romeo and Juliet*, and the Swan Queen in *Swan Lake*.

While most dancers who get these opportunities would have been making their debuts in their early twenties, I was thirty-two years old and performing these iconic roles for the first time in my career—I was making up for lost time. Although I was in great shape and felt strong, my body often reminded me that it was important to take even greater care of it than I had in my twenties. In the past I'd been able to go from season to season with ABT, then travel to perform as a guest with other companies and in dance festivals during hiatuses without missing a beat, but now that was less of an option for me. I needed to rest, as well as perform regular body rehab and maintenance. In addition, I worked on my artistic development, diving deeper into exploring the characters I'd be portraying in my upcoming ABT performances.

My age was not my only concern. I also had a surgically implanted metal plate in my shin, and the pain was fairly constant, even more so during ballets that required a lot of jumping and turning on that leg. In spite of these challenges, I was ready and determined to embrace these incredible opportunities.

I felt fulfilled artistically and was so focused on the continued recovery and management of my shin that promotions were not top of mind for me. In truth, I didn't even think about them until I could no longer ignore the buzz around my packed season of "firsts" and the retirement of three of our principal ballerinas: Julie Kent, Xiomara Reyes, and Paloma Herrera. In the press and on social media, everyone wondered who would fill their pointe shoes. The whispers about whether it would be "my turn" and whether I deserved the promotion at all grew louder. The scrutiny became intense, but I did my best to put my head down, block out the noise, and focus on the work ahead.

It wasn't until *Swan Lake* was approaching, in the seventh of an eight-week season, that the discussion around my promotion started to intensify and began to really take a toll on me. The questions in the public forum became, "If Misty fails in *Swan Lake* or doesn't execute things technically perfectly (they meant the fouettés), will she be promoted?" The nagging doubts I'd fought in Australia came back with a vengeance. *Could I be the ballerina?*

When approaching the role of Odette/Odile, I knew I wanted to get some guidance from Raven. Though she never pushed her opinions on me when it came to my process for roles, I made it a point to always listen attentively because I knew there would be nuggets of wisdom buried within her wit and humor. She often mentioned Alexandra Danilova, who had danced the Swan Queen with the Ballet Russe from the 1930s through the 1950s. Raven said hers was a beautiful interpretation. She also knew about my grappling with the thirty-two fouetté turns and shared that Danilova, one of the ballet greats, had avoided the turns altogether and opted for replacing them with a completely different step.

Raven also pointed me toward Maria Tallchief and Margot Fonteyn. These artists are from an era that celebrated ballerinas who danced their characters with complete abandon. Raven saw similarities in my and Maria's freedom in her signature role of the Firebird, and she explained how that freedom made her an even more powerful Swan Queen. With Raven's recommendations, I made sure I watched as many video clips of these iconic dancers as I could find. I also looked for my own inspiration, watching Natalia Makarova, Diana Vishneva, Julie Kent, Svetlana Zakharova, and so many more. The goal was to have a range of interpretations to pull from.

I didn't only focus on these dancers as Odette/Odile, but I also studied them performing the role of the Dying Swan in the ballet *Carnival of the Animals*. I felt that the way the swan finds freedom in her port de bras in the Dying Swan variation could be a useful tool to have as the Swan Queen. I focused specifically on Anna Pavlova's and Maya Plisetskaya's, two legendary Russian ballerinas, interpretations of the Dying Swan. They both gave beautiful and devastatingly wild performances in this role.

With all the inspiration I had in my head, it was Irina Kolpakova who brought it all into focus and turned it into a reality in my body. ABT's version of *Swan Lake* is Kevin McKenzie's choreography based on Marius Petipa and Lev Ivanov's version. Preparing for the ballet, I was coached and taught the choreography by Kevin, but in terms of style and finesse, it was all Irina Kolpakova. She drips with history and character and even in her eighties can demonstrate the exact nuance, grace, and flair required to portray every role in a ballerina's repertoire.

Irina had been the prima ballerina of the Kirov State Academic Theatre of Opera and Ballet (now the Mariinsky Theatre) in Saint Petersburg, one of the greatest Soviet-era ballerinas. She was in the last graduating class of Agrippina Vaganova, the founder of the Vaganova technique, one of the most popular ballet techniques to this day. It combined the elegant, refined style of the old French school, the beauty and smoothness of the arm movements of the old Russian school, and the strong and masterly feet technique of the Italian school. That was the background she was trying to instill in me.

She coached me on every detail from the tips of my fingernails down to the ends of my toes. Odette was incredibly different from Odile, both in character and in physicality. Odette is the hunted while Odile is the huntress. To Irina, the detail that really made all the difference between being good and being great was how I transitioned in and out of these two characters.

For Odette, the white swan, Irina brought my full attention to the idea of expansive legato dancing. Even if Odette is afraid, she should never get small in her demeanor. She broke down the undulation of the arms in specific detail, the movement originating from the back and expanding outward from the body with the placement of each finger precisely, creating a soft feathered end to the wing. My arm movements and positions were used to resemble taking flight, to take cover, and protect both me and my flock. Each move of Odette's wings expresses the emotion she's feeling; this is how she speaks and cries and screams. The ripple of the arms might appear fast and frantic, while other times slow and full.

Odile, the black swan, has a sharper, more staccato feel, with exciting and robust energy. Irina told me that when I'm holding the gaze of the prince under the evil sorcerer's spell, my eyes are looking deep into his soul with extreme intensity. When she demonstrated this for me, her small face lit up, her eyes widened, and her smile grew long and wide. We decided together exactly where in the room I would focus my eyes. The audience would see the whites in the corners of my eyes as I peered back at the prince, giving them the perfect angle to display the deceit in her character, to which he was oblivious. And at a moment's notice she would have me switch to the soft connected flow of Odette, luring him in with her soft and emotional warmth. These were details that would never be complete. Each time I take on this role, there's a deeper dive with Irina.

As the day of my New York debut approached, the pressures resulting from questions around whether I'd rise to the occasion, combined with the strain on my leg, became overwhelming. Or so it felt. For the first time, I started to feel debilitated in rehearsals for *Swan Lake*. Never in my entire career had nerves prevented me from executing steps, but the battle between my body and my mind was raging. Day after day, I tried and could no longer get through my fouettés in rehearsal. They were never a walk in the park for me after my surgery in 2012. In Australia, the fouettés were grueling, but they didn't come with the chatter and expectations of New York City balletomanes and the dance media. Now I can only describe it as my fouettés having simply vanished.

The stress fractures in my tibia had healed, but the screws

holding the plate in place continued to cause pain. My surgery leg is my left leg, which is my "turning" leg on which I perform the thirty-two fouettés. Any repetitive relevés, jumps, or anything causing impact made my shin swell, resulting in almost unbearable pain. What was most concerning to me was that I was letting outside judgment, the opinions of faceless strangers online and critics—some legitimate, some self-appointed—creep into my mind and process. I *knew* I was completely capable of executing the choreography and of totally letting go and becoming these characters, but now it was an expectation of failure that had me tripped up over the fouettés. Though this is by far the most difficult ballet in a ballerina's repertoire, physically, technically, and mentally, I knew I could do it. I *had* done it; and yet, for the first time ever in my career, my doubters were winning.

Raven's belief in me was unwavering, and her faith always led me back to what was important. She would remind me of the incredible opportunity in front of me, that I was about to perform *Swan Lake* on the Met stage to a house full of little brown girls and boys. I was about to take on a role that so many Black ballerinas before me could only dream of.

June 24, 2015. The day of the performance.

8:00 a.m. My alarm went off like a war horn for the battle of *Swan Lake* that lay ahead. It was different from how I had felt in Australia. It seemed more monumental to me. This was my home theater, the Met Opera, with the juxtaposition of my toughest critics and my most supportive and beloved fans and community.

9:00 a.m. As I entered the theater through the familiar backstage hallway, I reminded myself it wasn't my first time dancing the role in New York in this legendary space. Alex and I had performed the entrance and mime sequence for a very special show: *ABTKids.* A one-hour performance to introduce young audiences to the magic and beauty of dance.

So, I guess you could say my real *Swan Lake* debut happened one spring morning in 2014 at the Metropolitan Opera House in front of a house full of screaming kids, before I was ever cast to perform in the full production. Olu had taken the morning off from work to support me. After the performance, he shared how he was seated next to one young enthusiastic ballerina decked out in a tutu, brimming with excitement before my entrance, knowing a swan was about to take the stage. Tchaikovsky's score came to a dramatic build as I did a big jeté onto the stage, landing in a swan pose. As most of the audience welcomed me with applause, the girl yelled out, "Where's the Swan?!?" in complete disappointment. She continued to call for "the swan" throughout the course of my short five-minute performance. Apparently, she was hoping for an *actual* swan, so I guess I had more work to do on my interpretation.

Now I was facing a more ominous adult version of "Where's the swan?" Headlines like "Will Misty Copeland Be Promoted?"

and "Was Race a Determining Factor in Her Ascension?" were often really asking the questions "Could I be *the* swan? Did I deserve to be the swan? Did *any* Black woman?"

10:30 a.m. Company class. The ballet teacher led us through our barre exercises, the fundamental movements and essential building blocks preparing and warming us up to dance. I use the barre as a form of meditation, as class is my daily ritual. I was feeling anxious before class, but my body did what it knows and does best, gearing up for performance. Through class I got grounded and focused on the task at hand.

Noon. I sat in hair and makeup with James Whiteside, a new partner for me—it was our first full-length classical ballet together—trying to take in the moment. James has a beautiful way of keeping things real, and he reminded me to stay in the moment, that it was just ballet and we were going to have fun.

1:00 p.m. From hair and makeup I went straight to the stage, still in my warm-up clothes from class, to feel the floor, feel the energy, and really get centered. I tested out bits and pieces of choreography as the white swan. Just enough to get my body going but not enough to exhaust me. I leave the black swan's steps to go through at intermission.

I stepped into a series of arabesques that Odette executes in her opening entrance, using them to get me "on my leg" and find where my balance is. I went through the second-act variation in its entirety, "double ronde de jambe" to "relevé à la seconde," circling the leg as I rose to pointe with my leg extended high above my head to the side. This is one of the more difficult sequences of steps Odette does. Finishing the variation with a diagonal of stepover turns, ending in an iconic swan pose. And last, I acted out Odette's mime scene to really get into character to feel familiar and at home in the space. This is my one performance ritual: spending time behind the curtain. The stage alters your center of gravity, so this time is extremely important for me in order to get acclimated before every show. My head is completely in the game, focused on the steps and story with no distractions. I sync my mind and body, getting to a place of true calm and control.

1:30 p.m. Half-hour call. I headed to the corps de ballet dressing room, where I had chosen to stay after my promotion to soloist so that I could remain surrounded by most of my peers and some of my closest friends. In the crowded room of about thirty-five women, I slipped into my princess gown and touched up my makeup before making my way back to the stage. It was showtime.

1:59 p.m. In six minutes, the haunting horn sounds of the overture would begin, and the curtain would rise on a lakeside scene. After many well-wishes from my colleagues and staff, and Kevin and Irina, I stood stage right in the pool of blue light, as I had in Australia. This time Raven wasn't just the wind at my back. She was *there*, in the audience. I never think about who's in attendance before I perform, but this one was for her—especially for her. I took deep, slow breaths.

The energy in the audience was palpable. I could feel and hear it from the downstage right wing as if I were out there in the house. The curtain was being held because people were still entering the theater. I knew many of them were "my people," here to be a part of something bigger than all of us.

2:11 p.m. I stepped out onto the stage for the prologue, and the audience roared. Their energy pulsed through me; I knew everything was going to be all right.

2:35 p.m. It felt like a lifetime waiting through the first act, in which the prince celebrates his twenty-first birthday, to make my entrance as the swan in the second act. As I leapt out onto the stage, everything stood still. I had become *her*. James entered, and I felt his comfort and confidence. We were connected. The "love duet" felt like we were truly dancing in harmony with our bodies melding into one. He supported me in my pirouettes with his hands firmly and gently holding my waist, allowing for speed and dynamism that I couldn't accomplish on my own. He lifted me into the air with incredible ease, making me feel like I really might fly. I fell back into his arms with total trust, total abandon, the swan surrendering to her feelings for the prince. By the time he swore true love to me, his arm stretching toward the sky in an eternal vow, the audience went wild with applause.

3:05 p.m. Intermission—Irina rushed into my dressing room so pleased but staying cool, calm, and collected to not break my focus. She kissed me on the forehead and said everything went just as we rehearsed. She told me to keep on the same track for the third and fourth acts. I was in the midst of having my hair and makeup touched up when Irina turned her attention from my performance to the hair and makeup team. She let them know exactly what they needed to do to transform me into the black swan. Pointing out which bright-red lipstick color I would wear as Odile in the third act. She watched as they pinned my tiara on my head, then sent me on my way with her approval.

3:25 p.m. Going into the third act, I felt confident and in complete control. The "black swan pas de deux" in contrast to the "love duet" in the second act was full of excitement and desire. It felt effortless, thanks to James being incredibly engaged and grounded in his partnering. He gave me support, allowing me to fully commit to my character portrayal and be completely present and in the moment. I was in the zone as I tackled Odile's variation, but by the time the coda was taking place, the thirty-two fouettés got the best of me mentally and physically.

I approached center stage ready to whirl Prince Siegfried into a frenzy and was suddenly taken out of my zone. I was facing the audience dead-on, and my mind left my present body. I was Misty, not Odile. It was as if I could hear the naysayers already ripping my performance apart, and my surgery leg was exhausted and losing stamina. After only sixteen fouettés, I recovered with sixteen turns from fifth to finish. I always have a backup plan because, in the end, every bit of choreography is there to tell a story.

There are many choreographic variations of this moment that have existed since the ballet was created, which, later in my *Swan Lake* journey, I would commit to exploring, but the dazzle of the thirty-two fouettés over the audience has taken precedence.

The third-act pas de deux and variations are a buildup of lust and persuasion, culminating in a whirlwind movement that's supposed to stir up Prince Siegfried to completely blur his judgment and get him to swear to love the wrong swan, Odile, therefore breaking the promise he has to Odette, keeping her captive to the evil sorcerer forever. My goal in this section is to bring the audience into Odile's evil plan, allowing them to understand how the prince could have fallen under her spell.

But I was disappointed in myself for not getting through all thirty-two fouettés.

The third act came to a close and went right into the fourth act. I had to let go of my disappointment and move forward to a strong finish. The fourth act to me is not only a beautiful close to the ballet story, but personally, it's an incredible way to center myself after a long performance. It ends with Odette sharing a few more moments with the prince to express their love to each other before they both jump to their deaths to be together in the afterlife. As dramatic as this all sounds, it brings what can be a really stirring, emotional performance to a beautifully calm end. It elevates the ballet to an allegory of true love's immortality. Even though Odette doesn't get her wish in life, she achieves it in death as her soul unites with the prince's.

When the curtain rose and the company took our bows, I was back in my body, there with the audience feeling all the emotions. I could see the wings full of my colleagues, taking in the moment with me, including James and the whole cast.

And then Lauren Anderson, the Black ballerina legend whom I first saw on the cover of *Dance* magazine when I was seventeen years old, appeared from downstage right with a bouquet of flowers. Ballet tradition holds that bouquets are presented by men, typically ushers. To be presented a bouquet by a trailblazer who'd influenced my own career, during my *Swan Lake* debut at the Met, is a memory I will always hold dear. My heart exploded with pride as she lifted me in her arms and twirled me around. Lauren, the only Black ballerina I'd ever known to dance the full-length *Swan Lake*, was there on the stage with me. I couldn't believe what was happening. The next day she shared her thoughts:

You were awesome yesterday. Have you come down from the clouds?

When you do, remember that less is more in the 3rd act. You are already strong and can do everything!!!!! You can only give what you have, you don't have to be more than you are. YOU ARE ENOUGH!!!

Breathe OUT before the fouettés and relax in your plié.

You will really enjoy the next times you do it.

I kept telling Raven, I wanted to see the next one.

Thank you so much for including me in this special time in your career.

I heard her loud and clear. I was enough. We were enough!

And then came Raven. Watching her walk out onto the Metropolitan Opera House stage that day remains one of the absolute highlights of my career. She came out of the first wing, downstage right in the red dress that she wore for important occasions, holding a big bouquet of flowers. I immediately burst into tears. This wasn't about me; this was HER moment! The audience roared with admiration and respect for what she meant to me and to so many for whom she helped pave the way. It was as if my whole career had flashed before my eyes in that moment. All I could think to do was drop to one knee and bow to her. I'm *here* because of *her*. In her joy, she began to undulate her arms like wings. It was undeniable: we were *both* Swan Queens.

Once the curtain closed, I had a moment to speak with Irina and Kevin, and they were as proud as I was of this accomplishment. Debbie Allen, Judith Jamison, Stephanie Dabney (DTH's Firebird), and so many more Black luminaries had gathered in the Grand Tier of the house, where the moments just continued to feel even more unreal. Then Debbie Allen stood in the center of the crowd and spoke:

"We are living in a time where our nation is fractured, where we don't know who we are, where fear is our guide. And your performance today told us that there is hope, that there is something more that we can believe in."

I stood by Raven, and we held hands as we absorbed Debbie's words. Nearly fifty years separated us in age, but our journey, and this moment, which belonged to us both, made us one.

CHAPTER 10

DREAMS REALIZED

After the *Swan Lake* performance, still on a high, I met fans outside like I typically would after a show. But on this day, the crowd had grown so big that they had to be moved away from the cramped area outside the stage door to a space that could better accommodate such an enormous group.

At this point in my career, and more specifically this season, I was in a very peculiar position. With my growing profile in the media, and positive reviews in some of ballet's biggest roles, I was attracting large audiences and selling out shows. Yet I was still not a principal dancer. My unique journey showed how the media had changed and evolved in dance, certainly since Raven's era. Through the use of modern tools like social media and the brand partnerships that I had formed, my visibility had spread beyond traditional dance circles.

When I stepped outside the theater, the crowd cheered eagerly. A man shouted, "Principal! Principal. Misty for principal!" A woman called out, "Congratulations, Misty!" I couldn't believe how long they had all waited for me. It must have been over an hour since I stepped off the stage, greeted VIPs on the stage, and then the group in the Grand Tier. I was amazed and honored to see the long line of little girls and boys carrying their copies of my book *Firebird*, inspired by my friendship with Raven, and their parents holding copies of my memoir, *Life in Motion*, for me to sign.

Before signing autographs and posing for pictures, I took a breath, attempting to hold back tears, and said, "Thank you so, so much for your support. It means the world to me to have you all here. It's such a special day for me and for so many people who have come before me. So, thank you for being here on this amazing day."

Just as I wrapped up greeting the fans, one little girl got my attention, yelling my name as she said, "Thank you, Misty!" Her mom smiled as I turned around to see who this little one with the big voice was. The little girl's eyes widened as we looked at each other. Although I was on my way back inside the theater, I turned to walk back to her to give her a big hug. Moments like that, no matter how brief, can make the difference for someone—the difference between who she thought could be a ballerina before my performance and who she now knows is a ballerina after my performance. And that ballerina happens to also look like her. Her mom grabbed my hand to thank me for "seeing" her little girl. I was reminded: *This is for the little brown girls.*

The next day was a typical workday. Part of what I love about this art form is that it keeps you grounded. No matter how much praise you've received the day before, the next morning you have to get up and begin with the basics. First thing that morning I was in company ballet class, which I love taking after an important performance. It helps me to rebalance, getting me back to a place of symmetry both physically and mentally. A four-act ballet like *Swan Lake* is intensely brutal on the body and mind, and we're left to pull ourselves back together and prepare to do it all over again. After class I jumped right into rehearsals for the final ballet of the season, *Cinderella*, where I would dance one of the four fairies, the Autumn Fairy. This is a part of being a live performer. One ballet comes to an end, and another begins. We turn our attention to what we are doing at that moment and not what happened the day before, notwithstanding the headiness of the applause, the flowers at curtain call, the cheers of the crowd. On this day, I was no longer the lead, but a soloist again, supporting the rest of the cast to frame the principal dancers.

Though things moved ahead for the company, the public was even more curious than before as to what my future would hold at ABT, and it was expressed in the reviews following my performance. I did my best to take in all that had happened but decided to carry on with no expectations as the season wrapped up. I was excitedly preparing for the next big challenge in my career: Broadway. I would be taking on one of the female lead roles in *On the Town* in a couple of months, which required me to stretch my performance wings to include acting with a speaking role and singing live onstage. I had a huge learning curve ahead, but I was ready for the challenge. So, for me, it was business as usual at ABT until Tuesday, June 30.

A company meeting was held to review the Met season and discuss what was to come in the fall season ahead. Kevin sat in a folding metal chair at the front of the room, facing all of us. I sat on the floor, stretching, dressed in my rehearsal uniform: one of my far-too-old but extremely comfy leotards, tights, leggings, and a well-broken-in pair of pointe shoes. Without ceremony, Kevin began announcing promotions. My heart started to pound, but at the same time I felt oddly calm. After waiting through a long list of eight celebratory announcements of my peers' promotions, Kevin turned toward me and simply said, "Misty, take a bow." With those four words, I became a part of history as the first African American woman in ABT's seventy-five years to achieve the position of principal dancer. I had a flood of emotions, but mostly I was grateful to have risen to the occasion in a way that would make all the Black and brown bal-lerinas before me proud.

As happy as I was about this amazing news, I had to refocus and get to the next rehearsal of the day. I didn't have an oppor-tunity to call Raven for hours after the announcement. After my final rehearsal that day, I had about thirty minutes to pull myself together and to change into my street clothes. I was taken to the screening room, set up like a small movie theater in the Met Opera House, for an impromptu press conference to discuss the promotion. Dozens of journalists peppered me with questions. How did it feel? Did I ever believe it would happen? How did I plan to celebrate? What did I want to tell other young ballerinas trying to make it? Did I feel this would break the color line in ballet for good and make room for many more Black ballerinas? How did it feel to be *the first*?

As soon as I had a free moment, I stepped outside the stage door of the theater and into the garage of the Met, one of the few places I could get good cell service, and called Raven. She had heard about my promotion on the news and from all the calls she'd received from friends. The call was quick, and words weren't even really necessary. My internal dam broke, and the tears flowed down my face like a river unleashed. Raven and I cried together with a mutual understanding of what this moment meant. She said she saw beyond the technicality of the title and into the deeper meaning and weight of what it meant for us as Black people. This recognition was also for the long lineage of those whose shoulders I stand on and for the future representation of generations to come.

"I didn't think I'd ever see this in my lifetime," she said, her usually confident voice breaking. It filled me with immense gratitude and pride knowing I had given that to her.

Losing Her Religion

The years of touring with the Ballet Russe de Monte Carlo and the traumatic experiences in the South had left Raven exhausted, demoralized, and spiritually depleted. Though she rarely talked about religion, she was a woman of deep faith. So, she decided to join an Anglican convent in Fond du Lac, Wisconsin. The name of the retreat says it all: the "bottom of the lake." It was as if her experiences had left her so wounded that she needed to disappear, like the Swan Queen diving off the cliff when she cannot be with her true love on earth.

Raven's true love had always been ballet, and at that point it appeared she would not be "reunited" with it. Like Prince Siegfried in *Swan Lake*, her love had betrayed her. She needed to retreat to rediscover a purpose and understand God's plan for her life. She left New York and her family and moved to Wisconsin. Living among the nuns, with a set schedule regulated by prayer, simple meals, and long periods of silence and reflection, restored Raven's spirit.

This was one of many experiences that Raven and I bonded over. I had lived in a convent in Chelsea called the Carmelite Sisters when I first moved to New York. The El Carmelo Residence was an old five-story building with a steep winding staircase. The nuns accepted young women as boarders, and we all took our meals together at long tables in a cramped basement. Like Raven, I loved the peace, the order, and the kindness of the nuns.

Perhaps the life appealed to us both because ballet is itself a "calling." It stirs something deep within you when you encounter it as a child, and then you go on the ballet journey, wherever it may lead, giving up leisure time, "normal" relationships with friends and family, and regular school, to prepare yourself for your career. You have to be willing to devote yourself to it body and soul or you'll never excel in the art form. And your love for it, like faith, bolsters you through the days and nights of body aches and doubts that your efforts will lead you to be one of the "chosen" in a company.

Raven had followed her heart to the convent, but she had made no certain plans for her future. With no ballet career prospects and, other than her family and friends, no emotional ties to bind her, she felt lost. She trusted that if she waited and prayed, her "purpose" would eventually find her again.

Several months into her stay, a ballet company came to

South Bend, Indiana, to perform. Raven and her fellow nuns went to see them. Sitting in the theater, Raven felt the familiar thrill and deep emotion that had first been awakened in her when she saw *Coppélia* as a five-year-old at City Center. Like the Swan's love for Prince Siegfried, a ballerina's love for her art is true and eternal.

After the performance, Raven went backstage to see some of the dancers she knew. When she arrived in the dressing room, as she loved to recount, the ballerinas were milling around half-dressed, getting out of their stage costumes, laughing, cursing, and smoking. At the sight of Raven, who, in her full-on nun's habit, complete with veil and wimple framing her fresh and innocent face, must have looked like a saint out of a Renaissance painting, the dancers apologized for their foul language and cigarettes. They were certain they'd offended her. Raven burst out laughing and whipped off her veil, revealing her long, dark wavy hair. "Don't worry, girls," she reassured them, "I used to be one of you!"

Then, in typical Raven fashion, she sat down among the ballerinas, trading stories, asking them about their performances. That afternoon served as a reminder of her true identity: She wasn't a nun. She was an artist, a dancer. The next few weeks of reflection at the convent revealed to her what she'd known in her heart all along: dance wasn't done with her yet, and she wasn't done with dance. She had a gift, and it was a sin not to use it. Dance was *her* ministry.

Raven left that convent after six months and returned to New

York. Somehow, some way, she was going to get back onstage. She began by getting herself back into shape, taking classes every day, a tall order after a six-month forced "hiatus." This is a "climb" that I knew well, that every dancer knows. Injury and setbacks are part of any career. With Raven's and mine, though, the bodily fractures were compounded by very limited opportunities. Raven had auditioned for the Metropolitan Opera Ballet, where in 1951, they had accepted Black ballerina Janet Collins. Janet danced there until 1955, when she left. Raven was rejected in 1960.

Raven refused to give up. Finally, one day, by chance, she ran into her old friend and a School of American Ballet graduate, Sylvester Campbell. He had originally trained at the Jones-Haywood Dance School in Washington, DC, which was started by two Black women to accommodate all the ballet students the white schools wouldn't accept. A tall, elegant man with a gorgeous, chiseled face and café au lait complexion, Sylvester was often referred to as the "Black Nureyev." British dance critics described him as gifted with "a classical style of great purity, combined with fire, nobility, and all the other classical virtues."[1]

But in spite of his "danseur noble" qualities, Sylvester couldn't find a spot in an American ballet company. Arthur Mitchell ruled the stage as the first Black dancer at New York City Ballet, even partnering white women, a radical development. George Balanchine, founder and head of the company, refused to bow to pressure to have Arthur dance only solos to avoid "race mixing." But though Balanchine stood up for him, he brought no one else of color into New York City Ballet. For many years Arthur remained "the only." (Such tokenism has been a constant in the American ballet tradition. Looking back, many companies seemed until very recently to have a one-at-a-time policy for admitting Black dancers.)

Rejected in his own country, Sylvester had gone abroad and joined the Dutch National Ballet, where he was a star, dancing all the principal roles in the most iconic ballets: *Swan Lake*, *Giselle*, *Raymonda*, the canon. One afternoon in 1960, just as she'd returned from "the bottom of the lake," he and Raven ran into each other near the newly built Lincoln Center while he was in New York. He told her to come to Holland. And so she did.

She danced with the Dutch National Ballet for another ten years. Although Raven danced all the classics she loved, it's not a period of her life she ever talked about much. She was more likely to share a story of the Ballet Russe. In her heart of hearts, Raven, like her mother, considered herself an American. She enjoyed Europe and found the people very kind, but Holland just wasn't home.

Unlike artists such as Josephine Baker and James Baldwin, who preferred to live as expatriates, Raven missed America and her family. In 1974, thirty-eight years old and ready to retire from ballet, she packed her bags and came home, once again, not quite certain of what she would do next.

Sylvester Campbell, on the other hand, stayed in Europe,

going on to dance with Maurice Béjart and then to coach dancers for international ballet competitions in Moscow and Bulgaria. He would also serve as the competitors' partner and win honors. He finally returned in the early eighties to teach. He died relatively young, at fifty-nine, from respiratory ailments, with his *New York Times* obituary hailing him as a "pioneer." He had no surviving relatives. I can't help but wonder if Raven's decision to return home to her family and friends was what contributed greatly to her stamina, staying power, and constant joy. She was so full of energy and could outlast anyone at a party. Part of the secret was her family, even her parents, whose memory stayed so vivid for her long after they'd passed on. She carried them with her in her heart and honored their dignity in all that she did.

Considering Raven's longevity, I'm reminded that she surrounded herself with friends and made friends everywhere she went. She was endlessly curious about everyone around her, and she led a more active social life than I did when I was a single woman in my twenties. It was hard to get on her dance card! She could have written a book on aging well. Life didn't just happen to Raven; she created the life she wanted with intention.

Raven grabbed life with both hands and made the most of any moment. There was another secret to her joie de vivre: the occasional indulgence. One night, I went to our neighborhood liquor store. The man behind the counter said: "Hey, you're that dancer, right?"

"Yes, I am," I answered, always pleased to find a balletomane in unexpected places. I really didn't expect the warm but gruff man working the cash register at the liquor store on the Upper West Side to be an American Ballet Theatre fan.

"Your friend comes in here. Miss Raven. We love her!" he gushed, his eyes lighting up like a schoolboy with a crush at the thought of her. I had to laugh. Even the man working the local liquor store cash register had fallen prey to Raven's charms. I completely understood. With her huge eyes, her boundless energy, and her bright smile, Raven radiated warmth and love. She never failed to ask people how they were doing and actually waited—and cared—to hear the answer. The way she listened to you, you felt completely "seen and affirmed." You felt better about yourself and about life just being in her presence. I was so grateful she didn't stay in Europe, where her life might have been easier. If she had, so many who needed her here in the United States would not have had the chance to bask in her glow. That included the cashier at the local liquor store. And me.

Raven was so accessible and treated her groundbreaking achievements with such grounded humility that she taught me by example not to take myself too seriously. And to make certain there was always a little prosecco in the house to drink a toast to life.

CHAPTER 11

THE BELLS TOLL

The 2015 Met Opera season, a nonstop eight-week marathon of classes, rehearsals, dress rehearsals, and performances, ended on a beautiful note with the success of *Swan Lake* and my promotion to principal dancer. I was still on an incredible high that eventually became one of the longest comedowns from a performance I'd ever experienced. I was processing the most stimulating, pressure-filled seasons of my career. Everyone around me, especially Raven, breathed a sigh of relief from what was not only an exciting season but also a stressful one. Raven was there for and with me every step of the way, with countless phone calls of encouragement, numerous voice mails to inspire calm, peace, and confidence in the days leading up to each show, and a huge hug and whisper of congratulations backstage after each performance.

Traditionally, the spring season ends on the July Fourth weekend, and that year was no different. I was elated but completely exhausted and ready for my much-needed vacation with Olu to Santorini, Greece, to unwind before things picked up again full-speed ahead in only a week's time, in the run-up to my Broadway debut in *On the Town*.

The next day I had planned on sleeping in and packing for our trip, but Olu had other ideas. At the last minute he let me know that we would be meeting friends visiting from Singapore for dinner. After a couple of minutes of trying to negotiate a cancellation, I gave in and got dressed.

I must admit I was pretty annoyed and didn't hide it. The outfit I chose was a direct reflection of my displeasure. I wasn't happy, so I wasn't going to try to look good. I guess it was some sort of passive-aggressive punishment I was giving him. I put on my baggy cutoff jean shorts that had far too many holes in them, an oversize peach silk blouse that drowned my small frame, and a pair of his least-favorite trendy gladiator-style heels. He didn't seem bothered, which might have annoyed me more. We arrived at the Hudson Hotel near Columbus Circle, which held special meaning for us. Olu had surprised me there nine years earlier on my twenty-third birthday with a romantic staycation. But I still wasn't in the mood.

We went up the elevator to meet our friends in their room

for a glass of champagne before heading to dinner. Once we reached their room, he proceeded to take a key from his pocket and open the door. I yelled at him, "What are you doing? You should knock first. And why do you have a key?"

He opened the door, and the sounds of Sade's beautiful voice flooded the hall. I saw roses on the floor in the room behind him, and before he could say anything, I slowly started to back up and down the hallway, still in a bit of shock and confused that he had opened the door to our friends' room. This was no dinner with friends. It was all a ploy to get me here. He coaxed me back to the room.

Then he began talking about the journey of the last ten years. He emphasized how much we'd both grown as individuals and together and how much he admired the woman I'd become. He recalled how he had known when we first met, when I was twenty-one years old, that he would marry me one day. He knelt in front of me and pulled a ring box out of his pocket. I stood stunned. As he opened the box, revealing a beautiful diamond ring, he asked, "Misty, will you marry me?"

We'd been back together for two years, and our relationship was stronger than ever. The seven years we'd been together, then two and a half years apart, had shown me that there was only one Olu. His thoughtfulness and sensitivity were even evidenced in how he'd waited until after the season to propose, so as to not be a distraction in any way.

Still, I hadn't expected to be proposed to that night, after the unbelievable season I'd had, and certainly not in that outfit! But it was perfectly us. We'd seen each other through incredible ups and downs and had never felt more ourselves than when we were together. Olu had always been "home," and after so many years of turmoil and uncertainty in my life and career, I'd finally reached the point when I knew that was exactly where I wanted to be—with him, in the home our love created.

"Yes," I answered. It was the easiest and best "yes" of my life. The good times had always been easy and natural, but it was important that through every challenge, Olu had always been there for me, even when we weren't romantically involved. He didn't just tell me he loved me. He showed me every day by understanding what was important to me and "showing up," whether to a performance, in a crisis, or when I just needed someone to listen. I came to realize that Olu had always been my anchor.

Raven had loved him from the first day they met. Initially, she'd noticed how handsome and gracious he was, but more importantly, from early on in our friendship, Raven never missed an opportunity to point out how supportive he was and how rare that was to find in a partner, whether onstage or off. She'd make the comparison to the greatest dance partners, the ones who let you shine, the ones who made you feel so safe that you could take the risk, leap knowing they'd be there to catch you. In her eighty years, she'd seen so many women who'd either had to give up their artistic careers or give up on love because they couldn't find a partner who would allow them to blossom in both.

Raven had helped steer me back to Olu. She never lectured or told me what to do, yet in her sneaky but graceful way, she would point out his many acts of kindness. And, of course, when he was around, she would make eyes at him, singing his name, "Oluuuuuu," elongating the *u* so that it became a kind of love call.

She never talked about her own romantic life. Over the years, I met many of her dear friends, but to my knowledge she never introduced me to someone who had been a romantic partner. She was from a generation and grew up in an environment where people valued and respected privacy, so I never asked her. The great loves she would speak of were God, her family, and ballet.

The day after the hotel adventure, I called her to tell her Olu and I were engaged. "I can't wait to dance at your wedding!" she said, happiness dancing on her tongue.

And she did! A year later, in the summer of 2016, Olu and I had our official ceremony on the West Coast, where both our families lived. The following week, we held another celebration in New York for our East Coast friends on the roof of an art deco event space. Raven was the belle of the ball in an elegant black velvet dress, her salt-and-pepper hair swept up in its classic soft bun.

As she promised, in between glasses of prosecco, she took to the dance floor with Olu. She shared with him how happy she was for us and that she always knew he was the one.

It was such a beautiful New York midsummer night, with a picture-perfect sunset we could all admire from this glass box in the sky. We laughed, dined, and toasted. I felt like the luckiest woman alive. Little did I know, as I watched a beaming Raven dance with Olu, that it would be the last time I would see her in person.

CHAPTER 12

TAKING RAVEN'S BREATH AWAY

It was Thanksgiving 2016. Our wedding celebrations had ended, but the exciting and busy momentum of our lives had only ramped up. My first year as a principal dancer had been full and exciting with two New York City seasons, one in the fall and one in the spring, tours in between both periods with the company, and performances on my own as a guest artist as well. I had traveled to Los Angeles, Virginia, Montreal, Paris, the Maldives (for our honeymoon), Houston, Cuba, and finally ended up in Milan on my own for Thanksgiving, preparing for shows of *Romeo and Juliet* with La Scala Ballet. Raven and I always made a point of speaking around that special holiday. She would say to me, "This year, I'm grateful for you." Raven was an irreplaceable source of unconditional love. Even though I didn't get to see her as often as I would have liked, I felt her love and support in everything I did.

"What are you doing for Thanksgiving?" I asked her.

"I'm going to be with my family in Washington, DC!" she answered cheerfully. I never suspected anything was wrong. Her voice on the phone was strong, upbeat, and vibrant. I returned from Milan and went straight into rehearsals with ABT for that year's *Nutcracker* season at the Segerstrom Center for the Performing Arts, in Costa Mesa, California. Raven's calls were infrequent, but I assumed it was because she was out and about. Even at eighty, she had a very full life of social events, friends to see, and performances to attend.

One day, early in December, Gilda reached out to Raven just to see how she was doing. The truth came out. She confessed to Gilda that during her Thanksgiving visit to her family, one of her cousins who was a physician had noticed the difficulty she had breathing. He'd made her promise to see a doctor when she returned to New York.

She kept her word and had just been diagnosed with COPD, chronic obstructive pulmonary disease, a lung disease that limits your airflow and causes shortness of breath. Though Raven had given up smoking many years before, the damage to her lungs had caught up with her. As the disease progressed, everyday activities— walking to the grocery store, going out to a restaurant—became almost impossible. Raven told Gilda she didn't want to worry me.

She knew Gilda's father suffered from COPD, so she didn't have the same hesitation in sharing the news with her.

Being the strong, proud woman she was, Raven never wanted pity. In our relationship, she was very comfortable giving me love and support. To my continual frustration, she was less comfortable receiving any help from me. The last thing she wanted was to be a burden.

We continued to speak regularly over the next few months. I knew she did not want to discuss her health, so I respected her wishes. As usual, she wanted to hear *everything* about my travels, my performances in Milan as Juliet with the incomparable Roberto Bolle, a star of La Scala who looks like Michelangelo's statue of David come to life. She was also excited to talk about preparations for my new role as Giselle, another tragic Petipa classic and another milestone for a Black ballerina.

When the 2017 spring Met season came, the publisher of *Trailblazer: The Story of Ballerina Raven Wilkinson*, a children's picture book illustrating Raven's life, gifted Raven with orchestra seats to attend all my spring performances. But for the first time since I'd known her, Raven didn't come. And she never let me know she wasn't coming. We'd learn at intermission or at the end of the performance, when she was nowhere to be found.

She was really excited about my *Giselle* debut, so Raven and I made arrangements for her to attend. I held out hope that she'd get to see at least one performance, but at the last minute she canceled. Again, not wanting to cause me distress, she made light of it and hid her worsening condition. But I knew it was more serious than she would admit. Aside from her unflagging support of me, *Giselle* was one of her favorite ballets. She'd often shared how moved she was by Alicia Alonso's performances in the role at the Ballet Russe de Monte Carlo. Missing my debut—a Black ballerina's debut in this role—was completely out of character for Raven.

It was clear she was spending more and more time cooped up in her Upper West Side apartment. The COPD had advanced to the point that moving around was a huge challenge. She'd become tethered to her at-home oxygen tank. Raven's excuse for no longer getting out was that she couldn't breathe without her oxygen.

Gilda and I discussed that a solution could be a portable oxygen tank. The challenge was that Raven was a very petite woman. I'd be surprised if she weighed a hundred pounds, which was her natural size. Carrying around a portable oxygen tank, which typically weighed six to seven pounds at that time, could be a drain for Raven, who was already struggling with breathing.

We decided if we could find a portable oxygen tank that was compact enough, she could get back to her busy social schedule. And hopefully she could join me at performances and dinner at our favorite restaurant, Café Luxembourg. I truly missed her.

After a lot of research, we found the Inogen. It was the size of a purse and weighed only two pounds. It was a stealth operation because Raven refused any help from anyone, and she never, in all the years we knew her, let us visit her at home. Very few friends ever got beyond the lobby of her building. When Gilda, with whom she spoke more openly about her condition, would ask her how she was getting her medication, or her food, she'd brush her off with a cheerful "These days, you can get anything delivered. Even wine!" But if we could just get that Inogen machine to her, I thought, we'd have our Raven back.

We'd need a prescription from Raven's doctor to order the machine, so we had to concoct a plan in order to get ahold of her doctor without her finding out about our scheme. Gilda spoke with Raven and told her she was bringing her father, who was also suffering with COPD, to New York and needed to have a medical team in place in case he needed it. Raven happily gave her the doctor's contact information. When Gilda called, the doctor reminded her that HIPAA prevented him from giving her any information. Gilda explained that I was trying to buy her an Inogen machine so she could get back to her life. In the end, he spoke with Raven without divulging that it was us behind the oxygen caper and wrote the prescription. We bought the machine. I was thrilled. I could see her again! Or so I thought.

Upon receiving it, Raven was not pleased with Gilda for tricking her into sharing her doctor's name. Nor was she pleased that we'd paid for it without her permission. Once she calmed down, she laughed as she admitted that it was impressive that we'd gotten it done.

But that's about as far as we'd get. Mission was not

accomplished. The machine sat uncollected in her building package room. We all offered to go over to her apartment and help her set it up, but she wouldn't hear of it. When she and I did speak over the phone, she continued to downplay the severity of her condition, saying she wouldn't come outside with the portable breathing machine because she was embarrassed.

Since she never let me come to her home throughout all the time we'd known each other, I would beg her to meet me at Café Luxembourg. She would promise "next time, next time," in a cheerful tone of voice. But "next time" never came. It was frustrating for all of us who loved her and wanted to be there to help her not to be allowed "in." But that was the way she wanted it. I knew she operated by the stoic code of "Black elders": "You're the baby; you'll never see me sweat, and I'll never show you the depths of my pain." That didn't mean I didn't know it was there.

It became more difficult to reach her on the phone. I would have to let her home phone ring sometimes ten to fifteen times because that's how long it took for her to get to it with her diminished breathing. And if she answered, I could tell how out of breath she'd be just getting from one place in her apartment to the next. I tried to be more strategic about when I called because I did not want her to rush herself or suffer with her breathing just because I was calling to check on her.

Instead, I wanted to go pound on her door and tell her to let me in, to let me help her. I wanted to beg her, "Please don't lock me out. I love you. I need you." But there were boundaries

I knew not to cross because doing so would only cause her more pain. I had to give her the dignity of having her space. Just as Eleanor, her roommate in the Ballet Russe, couldn't cross the racial line and follow her to the "Colored hotel," I couldn't breach the line of privacy that separated us. So, slowly, she faded from my reach. I felt I was losing her, but I wouldn't let it cross my mind that one day soon she'd truly be gone.

CHAPTER 13

TRANSITION

In the spring of 2018, I was entering a new phase in my journey. I had been a principal dancer for three years and was coming up against another wave of uncertainty, feeling I must fight to prove myself to the ballet world as I once again dealt with some very public scrutiny around my *Swan Lake* performances. Raven was not very present in my life at that time, as she was holed up in her apartment dealing with her health issues, which I know contributed to the precariousness I felt in my own life. She'd been my rock. I was scared for her, and truthfully, that made me scared for me.

It all started in March 2018, while ABT was on tour performing *Swan Lake* at the Esplanade Theatre in Singapore. An audience member filmed the third-act coda of my performance as Odile, the black swan, on their phone. It was not my best performance. Already dealing with feelings of shame and embarrassment around that show as my own worst critic, once I returned home to New York City, I would see that the person had posted the video to YouTube titled "Misty Copeland's Fouetté Fail," putting a cherry on top of an already incredibly low moment for me.

After a couple of days spent reflecting on my feelings, I decided to post the video to all my social platforms.

I'm happy to share this because I will forever be a work in progress and will never stop learning. I understand my position, what I represent, and I know that I have been given a rare platform, which I've hoped to use to bring ballet to more people.

Further, I believe that ours is a subjective art form that does not lend itself to anointing the "best ballet dancer," nor is that my goal. I strive only to be the best ballet dancer that I can be. I've worked extremely hard to be where I am, and I hope that what I bring to the table is authentic artistry based on my particular point of view and life experiences. I never envisioned myself as the Swan Queen after being in the company for almost fifteen years before I was given the opportunity. I have such deep and conflicting feelings connected to

Swan Lake. As a Black woman and as a ballerina given the chance to take on this role.

For a variety of reasons, I often question if I deserve to perform this role. My conclusion is I do.

People come to see ballet for the escape. For the experience of being moved through our movement and artistry, not to score us on the technicality of what we do. This is why ballet is not a sport.

A ballerina's career is not, nor should be defined by, how many fouettés she executes. The turns are a part of the choreography to tell a story of pulling off the entrancement she holds over Prince Siegfried. The point is to finish the third act with a whirlwind movement that sucks him in just one last time before it's revealed that Odile is not Odette. This is the incredible beauty of ballet. To tell stories through dance and to hopefully move people. And that is an incredible opportunity that I will never take for granted.

I felt this was an opportunity to open the complicated dialogue about where we are as a society within ballet culture, the judgment that comes with being in the public eye, the integrity of our craft, and the sacredness of what it means to perform in live theater.

At the same time I took it upon myself to see what I could

learn from the criticism I was seeing online to grow as a dancer. I concluded that some of the technical difficulties I was experiencing were the result of the lingering pain in my tibia, which continued now six years post-surgery. I hoped the pain could be ameliorated by reassessing my training and technique. I had done this many times throughout my career after major injuries. In 2012, while recovering from the initial surgery, I found a floor barre teacher and a new approach to cross-training that would work for me at that time. Here I was, yet again, at thirty-five years old, retraining my body.

Raven hadn't attended a single performance during my 2018 ABT spring season, and I was feeling lost and uneasy without her presence. I decided to begin private training during the season, and in this time of feeling out of control, I found a new ballet teacher. The work began. I dove in headfirst, no longer taking daily company ballet class as I had my entire career, but now solely taking private lessons with this new teacher. I needed to prove to myself that it was never too late to work toward becoming the dancer I wanted to be.

And then, on December 17, my world was flipped upside down. Raven died.

Gilda had received a call from Denise Saunders Thompson, director of the International Association of Blacks in Dance, telling her the news. I was in California for ABT's annual *Nutcracker* performances when I was awakened early in the morning with a knock on my hotel room door. I was confused to see my partner and close friend Blaine Hoven at the door. I knew something must be wrong. I hadn't had my cell phone ringer on, so I had missed all the calls from Gilda. I asked with a bit of panic, "What's going on?" He just handed me his phone. Gilda had called him and let him know Raven had passed away. She wanted me to find out from her and not from reading it online. She also didn't want me to be alone when she told me.

Hearing Gilda say, "Misty, Raven passed away today," shattered my heart. Even though I knew her health was fragile, just knowing she was there was a source of comfort and strength. Her death left a hole no one else could or would ever fill. And I couldn't help but think about what I might have done to help her, of the moments we might still have had if she had let me in.

Now it was too late. She was gone.

For the first time in my twenty-year career, I canceled my rehearsal. I had no steps in me. Only pain. And questions. Why had she died alone? Had I told her and shown her how much I loved her? Had I thanked her enough for all that she'd brought to my life? Why couldn't I have had just one more month, week, day, hour to ask her everything I wanted to know? Just to hear her voice. She had lived eighty-three years, but it wasn't enough. I wanted more; the world wanted and needed more.

I have often found it difficult to strike a good balance in my life between my professional career, my personal life, and public obligations. And as dancers, we are both professional athletes and artists. The physical commitment to training our bodies day in and day out, combined with the emotional vulnerability needed to hone our artistry, takes incredible sacrifice as well as an enormous toll. As a principal dancer, these demands can take precedence over other things in life. This comes with enormous guilt that made me look back at my time with Raven and think, *How did I miss this? Was I just too busy? Was I not present enough?*

Several days later, I ran into Kevin a few blocks from the theater as I was heading to rehearsal. He gave me a warm hug and said, "I'm so sorry for your loss. I see how much Raven contributed to your growth. She helped you blossom. You'll never lose that." With all Kevin and I had been through in twenty years, his words touched me deeply. He had obviously seen her impact, and I felt his compassion as he looked at me.

And he was right. I didn't have Raven anymore, but no one could take away all the love she had poured into me. I made certain to bring that love to the performances I gave days after her passing in one of my favorite roles, Clara in *The Nutcracker*. Onstage that night, I let Raven's joy for life and ballet shine through me. She had danced *The Nutcracker* many times in her years with the Ballet Russe but never as the lead. On that night, I danced the principal role for both of us and to honor her memory.

Since I'd first met Raven, I'd resolved to use my voice to make her story known. Her passing only strengthened that commitment. Feeling such loss, the only thing I could think to do was to celebrate her life. Gilda and I organized a memorial service on March 25, 2019, at Abyssinian Baptist Church, the legendary house of worship in Harlem where Raven had grown up.

In front of a loving audience of 150 of her eclectic range of friends and dance luminaries, a heartfelt tribute was performed. Erica Lall, Courtney Lavine, and Calvin Royal III, three of five Black dancers in ABT, danced to pay tribute to the woman who had helped make our careers possible. Speeches were made by many luminaries, including Zita Allen, Delores Browne, Nelson George, Sandra Fortune-Green, Virginia Johnson, and me.

I spoke directly from my broken heart:

I've been at a loss for words anticipating this day and this very moment. But as I accept loss and try to understand why Raven was brought into my life, the more I see today as just the beginning.

I can't thank you all enough for being here to celebrate one of the most incredible people I've ever known: Raven Wilkinson.

From the moment I learned of this angel, my mission in life became unbelievably clear: to share her, and by extension, our story, with the world.

I know that her life's work, commitment, and dedication to ballet is what we all see, know, and appreciate. Her willingness to put so much at risk just to be able to experience the incredible beauty that ballet brought her. Her tenacity and strong will shined through with such dignity, honor, and clarity. But getting to know the woman behind the ballerina was even more unbelievable.

Raven had an unexpected and racy sense of humor that would leave me doubled over in laughter. Her uncanny ability to remember the most detailed stories and never repeat the same one twice. She shared her pure heart, support, and encouragement with me day after day. Reminding me time and again that she would always be the wind at my back.

And her words will live on within me every day, and her spirit will dance with me on every stage. Raven was genuine, caring, and loving. No matter what was happening in her life, she was thinking of others.

I know that the last year of her life was extremely difficult. I can relate to her stubbornness and need to do things in her own way. On all the phone calls we shared those last months, she insisted on talking about the trivial problems I was having in my life rather than what she was going through.

What allows me to rest easy is holding on to the last conversation we had this past July.

I expressed to her with this odd sense of urgency I had been experiencing that I needed to know *everything* about her life that she hadn't shared with me. I cried and cried and told her that I would forever share her life and the stories of all the Black dancers whose shoulders I stand on with the world. I asked her to please start writing things down, and in Raven fashion, she giggled and said, "Oh, Misty, you can just record our calls." I laughed and laughed. I hung up the phone with a big smile on my face, with a sense of pride, contentment, and love.

Raven showed me what it is to be a selfless, elegant, and strong Black woman. Your body is no longer with us, but your unbelievable spirit will never leave.

You embodied what it is to be a leader and a game changer. You fought for my future, and I will forever fight for the future of all of those watching me.

You will live on in every brown girl and boy who has the beautiful responsibility and privilege of experiencing this incredible art form.

Ballet brought us together and bonded us in a way that nothing else could have. I love you, and you will forever be the wind at my back.

You Can Go Home Again

Raven's journey was full of serendipity and coincidences straight out of a classic novel. It was 1974, and she'd been back in the United States for just a few weeks when she happened to take a stroll on the beautiful Lincoln Center Plaza. This was one of her favorite spots in all of New York, and it remains mine. There's nothing like walking up the marble steps toward the fountain, the David Geffen Hall rising on your right, the David H. Koch Theater on your left, and right in front of you, the majestically arched windows of the Metropolitan Opera House, revealing its thirty-foot Chagall paintings, made specially by the artist for the house when it opened.

As Raven circled the fountain and walked past what was then known as the New York State Theater, she thought, *I've always wanted to perform here. Oh well, it's probably too late.* Then, again, purely by chance, she ran into a friend who worked with the New York City Opera Company, which had given the

Black opera singer Camilla Williams her debut as Cho-Cho-San in *Madame Butterfly* in 1944. Raven's friend told her they were looking for dancers for the opera company and that she should join them. A few days later, Raven did.

Her good friend and fellow City Opera dancer, Candace Itow, recently described the first time she saw Raven onstage. She was dancing in the City Opera corps in a scene in the tragic opera *La Traviata*. "I couldn't take my eyes off her. She didn't have a solo. It wasn't a featured role, but she was the one who drew your attention," Candace said. That was in 1974. Soon thereafter, Candace met Raven and learned her story. As dancers in the opera company, they were responsible for taking their own daily ballet classes. The two went to ABT's company classes, which, at the time, were open to other artists. They'd routinely find themselves at the barre beside the great stars of the era, like Natalia Makarova and dancers from the Royal Ballet or the Bolshoi when they were in town. This must have been heaven for Raven and brought back the glory days of the Ballet Russe, when she trained daily beside the greatest ballet dancers of her day.[1]

Candace and Raven roomed together when the company took its annual trip to Los Angeles, and the two women bonded over their similarly doting fathers. Raven's father even performed a root canal on Candace. And as the two friends walked around New York after rehearsals or performances, Raven would regale

Candace, who had grown up on the West Coast, with New York history and tales of her mischievous childhood. Once when Raven's mother arrived at the Ethical Culture School to pick her up wearing a new hat, Raven cheekily asked, "What's that bucket on your head?" Mrs. Wilkinson was far from amused and let her daughter know. Like me, Candace rejoiced in the unexpected naughtiness of this angelic, elegant woman.

She was known and loved by everyone from the stagehands to the directors, to Beverly Sills, the great opera diva and the company's artistic director in the eighties. Many in the company didn't know about her history with the Ballet Russe until an article appeared in a *Dance* magazine in the nineties, and a member of the administration posted it for all the company to see. Their reverence for Raven only grew.[2]

The New York City Opera is where Raven finished her dancing career, dancing in operas until 1980, when she became one of their character actors. She stayed with them until 2011, the year the company folded and the year she and I met.

You couldn't walk past or into the Koch Theater with Raven without her being stopped every few feet by a security guard, a ticket taker, a stagehand, all who knew and loved her. She created a community everywhere she went.

The essence of her magic was the same quality she brought to her performances: She made people feel good about life and about themselves. She made people feel connected to each other and to her. Though she never danced on the Metropolitan Opera House stage, like so many brilliant artists who have graced Lincoln Center's spaces, she contributed to its greatness. She is an intrinsic part of the structure, an indelible part of its history.

And each time I take the stage at the Met, her spirit is with me.

BLACKFACE, RACIAL RECKONING, AND RAVEN'S WISH

There was a bleakness to 2019. I was struggling to find my legs. Raven was gone, and I was attempting to learn a different ballet technique than I had known. I had completely lost my balance. The year went by without my having a real grasp on what the outcome of this retraining experiment would be. The training was a much more in-depth approach than I'd previously taken post-injury or ever in my career. I typically would add different forms of cross-training to my regimen, but now I was learning a whole new way of dancing from the ground up.

Similarly to a lot of American-trained ballet dancers, I have learned an assortment of techniques by way of a handful of teachers whose backgrounds came from influences from the Royal Academy of Dance (RAD), the English style, and its merging of Italian, French, Danish, and Russian techniques. Maggie Black, who had developed a ballet style based on anatomy. George Balanchine, whose approach was to utilize more space in less time, which results in increased speed, height, and length. I would be retraining solely in the Vaganova technique, the same that Irina Kolpakova had been trained in. The Vaganova method highlights expressiveness of port de bras, where all parts of the arm (from hand to elbow to shoulder) are important, extreme flexibility, but in an artful way, and a mobile lower back. Dancers trained in this technique are taught to be strong and clean without stiffness.

And I was doing so while still going onstage and performing in front of a live audience. I felt like a colt, learning to walk, except I was on the world stage with thousands of people watching.

By the time the spring season had arrived, I felt I had more of a grasp on how to utilize my newfound training and channel it into *Swan Lake*, which had been the motivation to make this change in the first place. Raven was in my thoughts and kept me pushing through to become the swan that I wanted to be. I took to the stage as the Swan Queen with a newfound confidence alongside ballet superstar David Hallberg. This was a familiar partnership, as we'd been friends since we were seventeen years old in ABT's Studio Company.

The performance felt like a new beginning for me, full of optimism and excitement. I would get a chance again, weeks later, with another familiar partner, Herman Cornejo, at the Wolf Trap National Park for the Performing Arts in Virginia. That performance has been my best *Swan Lake* experience to date. I was in complete control and had embraced my own version of who I wanted her to be. I could feel Raven with me, and I knew she was proud. These balletic accomplishments provided some solace as I mourned the loss of Raven. She was always with me when I took the stage, but it was the strength she provided offstage that would help me get through what came next.

Then in December 2019, while ABT was on tour in Orange County, California, performing *The Nutcracker*, I was approached by some of my Black colleagues who brought a disturbing social media post to my attention. Two dancers from the esteemed Bolshoi Ballet Academy in Russia had posted an image of themselves on Instagram covered from head to toe in black makeup, revealing the Bolshoi's practice of using blackface in the theater's production of the classical ballet *La Bayadère*. This practice has been abandoned in recent decades by ballet companies in the United States, but the Bolshoi and the Mariinsky in Russia still use blackface in their productions today.

Raven immediately came to my mind when I saw these images. I wondered what she must have felt seeing the same and much worse throughout her life and career. Though I'm aware of the slow-to-change state of ballet culture, it's still devastating to see that there could be no sensitivity or understanding of how an entire community is affected by revisiting a hurtful history steeped in centuries of racism. But most disappointing was how little had changed since Raven had been a dancer.

I believe that as students, dancers, and leaders representing cultural institutions like the Bolshoi Ballet, we have a responsibility, especially with the visibility and reach we have through social media, to uphold a standard of integrity and inclusion. This was not something I could overlook. So I reposted the photo to my social platforms with a caption that read "This is the reality of the ballet world." Within seconds of posting, I was hit with an avalanche of attacks from Russian trolls calling me a monkey and every other racist name in the book, as well as a hit piece from the state-run Russian newspaper. The artistic director of the Bolshoi Ballet, along with some of the company's star dancers, responded in defense of their actions by saying that blackface is not offensive in their history or culture and that they refused to stop using it.

In the midst of these attacks, I was asked by Kevin, my artistic director, to apologize to the Bolshoi for causing such an uproar. I was dumbfounded. He was a kind, sensitive man, and yet he didn't seem to understand what he was asking of me. As the first and only Black female principal dancer at ABT, I couldn't apologize for taking a necessary stand against blatant racism.

The lack of support I felt throughout the company as my peers completely ignored the situation in the days that followed left me feeling utterly abandoned. This isolation reminded me of how I've felt so often throughout my career: alone. My fellow dancers and the ballet community couldn't understand my experiences as a Black woman in the world and in ballet, and not having Raven to talk to made everything even more difficult. I had so many things I wanted to ask her. How had she stayed so positive amid so much adversity? Where did she find the strength to continue?

The story was eventually picked up by many major publications here in the United States, and the ballet community went into cleanup mode. A lot of the conversation shifted from the situation at hand to getting rid of or tweaking existing ballets. Classics like *La Bayadère, Le Corsaire,* and *The Nutcracker,* which carry so much racism and sexism in their history, were reassessed. Getting rid of or altering these ballets is certainly a start, but it isn't going to address the underlying issues or meaningfully educate people. We must look further and discuss why blackface is not acceptable, its ugly history, and how it was used to dehumanize Black people the world over in support of slavery and then Jim Crow in the United States. It is time to explore why ballet struggles to include Black dancers, nearly a hundred years after it was first introduced in America. Only then can we start to make effective change.

The combination of losing Raven and the Bolshoi blackface debacle made me feel even more of a responsibility to continue to push the conversations about racism in ballet forward.

Before I knew it, the pandemic, the Black Lives Matter movement uprising, and the murder of George Floyd all came to a head at once in 2020. And it all collided with my own personal frustrations, doubts, fears, and crossroads in ballet. Am I truly making an impact? Is ballet really a safe and prosperous place for dancers of color to be? Things were bubbling over and eventually exploded.

A racial reckoning was underway, and the ballet world was ripped at its seams. We were forced to address hundreds of years of exclusion and racism, as well as how we would remain relevant with our livelihood now being taken away, with theaters dark all over the world as a result of COVID-19. No longer together in company class and in studios for rehearsal, we began to have virtual conversations about what needed to change and evolve in ballet while meeting from our living rooms, kitchens, home offices, and bedrooms.

As the summer of 2020 wore on, theaters and studios remained closed, and the world was still largely shut down. We were left to pick up the pieces and start anew. First, ABT addressed these very "in your face" issues in our internal company meetings in which I bared my soul and shared instances of racism that I'd experienced throughout my career and, more specifically, in the recent year. I expressed my hurt and frustration with the lack of support I felt from my colleagues and the ballet community when taking on the Bolshoi on my own. It's an experience Raven must have felt a million times over throughout her career.

Now was our chance to learn from our past, reflect on the lives of dancers from generations like Raven's, and evolve. To learn to be a support system for everyone within the ballet community, not just for those to whose experiences you could most easily relate. For the first time, my Black colleagues felt empowered to join me in speaking about their own challenges, and for the first time, it felt like we were being heard. This was a new leaf.

The arts and ballet organizations and institutions eventually followed suit, asking for me and many of the dancers of color in the ballet community to speak on panels and lead discussions about race. I opened the first panel I would participate in with these words:

In the larger picture of what's taking place in the world right now, I acknowledge that dance is only a small portion of the conversation about systemic racism, but in MY eyes, it is an important one, as the institution of ballet reflects the very systems that are now being railed against.

Mainstream ballet companies are somewhat unique in today's world in that, instead of exploiting Black or brown people, as is the case in many industries, we have simply been excluded. Further, many ballet companies hide behind the intended consequences of the systems designed to limit people of color's access to things like funding, exposure, training, and equipment to justify this exclusion.

At this very moment we are at a pivotal point in history, when the conversation of racial injustice is again at the forefront. It made me ask myself, "What is my role as a Black woman? What is my role as a ballet dancer? And what is my role as a Black woman in ballet?"

Throughout my twenty years at American Ballet Theatre, this discussion has become my life's work. It is easy for me because my experiences as a Black ballerina and a Black woman in America so closely mirror each other.

There are varying forms of privilege in the world that we ALL need to be mindful of and empathetic to. I acknowledge that being biracial or lighter skinned is a privilege both in the world and in ballet. But at the end of the day, I am unapologetically a Black woman, and my complexion does not exclude me, or anyone who looks like me, no matter the shade, from discrimination in either space. So I have used my platform to speak out about the lack of diversity and inclusion in ballet, sometimes to people's displeasure, but I made a decision a long time ago that I refuse to be silent. Silence does not bring about change.

I am here through hard work and the fight of those who came before me, through every Black dancer who was told no, that they weren't good enough, that they didn't have the right body type, that they didn't have the right skin tone, that they could never be the Swan Queen, the Firebird, Kitri, Coppélia, Giselle, Juliet, and Clara... that they could never be a classical ballerina.

I am proud and humbled to be here today to say none of that was ever true; that's just what they wanted you to believe. That's why every time I have the privilege to take the stage as a principal dancer, those who came before me take the stage, too. My very existence in this space is a tribute to groundbreaking ballerinas like Joan Myers Brown, who is with us today. Thank you, Joan, for all that you have done and continue to do today to make sure our faces are seen, our voices are heard, and our bodies are included on the stage.

I also had the privilege to touch the hand and heart of history, getting to know Raven Wilkinson, who mentored me as both a ballerina and a Black woman. As a Black ballerina in the 1950s, Raven came face-to-face with the perils of very overt and direct racism, so much so that she eventually had to leave her company in order to protect her life and to leave this country in order to have a career. I had the opportunity to learn from her, to be inspired by her, to be motivated by her. Times like now make me ask, "What has changed in all these years?"

Certainly, some things have improved. There are more dancers of color in more companies than ever before. At my company, Calvin Royal III, a soloist, and I were cast to perform the lead roles of Romeo and Juliet this spring, another historic milestone in ballet.

But we have so much more to do, so much further to go. The day I hope we will all see is when a ballet performance with two Black lead dancers is no longer a historical marker. It should be, as it is with any other dancer who has the great opportunity to perform an iconic lead role, another eagerly anticipated, wonderful afternoon or evening at the ballet to see great beauty and artistry on the stage.

The day I hope we will all see is when the story is not that a Black choreographer created a piece for a classical ballet company. Instead, the story is purely about the artistry of what was created and what makes the piece unique and exciting.

The day I hope we will all see is when there are Black artistic directors, Black costume designers, Black production professionals, and Black executive directors at the highest levels of classical ballet. Not just because they're Black but because they have the experience, the talent, the commitment, the vision, the passion, the excellence...because they earned the opportunity.

How do we make that happen? How do we make equality in dance a reality and not just a dream or an aspiration?

It's going to take more than just one voice, or even the six voices on this panel. It takes the work of all of us. That's why today's discussion gives me hope. Yes, we on this panel are the ones talking, but what's even more important is you're here listening. You see us. That is a start.

Now, at thirty-nine years old and after twenty years with ABT, I have a very different outlook on life, the ballet community, and how I fit into it. I understand my responsibility and the weight of my words. My son, Jackson Omri Evans, entered the world on April 2, 2022. I experienced what every new parent does: the cracking open of my heart to a new level of boundless love. I watch him yawn and ball up his tiny fists as he drifts off to sleep in my arms, and I want to make certain that one day, he awakens to a better world than the one we've known. I want not only to be the wind at his back but also to give him wings that will allow him to pursue his biggest dreams one day. His birth has only renewed my determination to help finish the work generations of African Americans began.

In spite of all the work left to be done, I feel a sense of peace knowing that in a post-Raven world, we are moving in a positive direction with a sense of hope for a more just society that is being held accountable for its actions. Though I wish Raven could have seen me become a mom and continue to fight for others to have opportunities she never had, I know she would be so proud seeing me tell not just her story but the stories of so many like her.

Raven's impact feels so alive and directly connected to the conversations we're having about race today and to the work being done to evolve ballet into a more inclusive and diverse art form. With her incredibly positive view of the world, I feel like she's left a little bit of her stardust behind. As I recall from the magical night I met Raven, over ten years ago, she said that life is an ensemble effort, our culture is, and we have to endeavor to work together.

Raven's story continues to resonate with so many and will continue to inspire generations to come. Every little brown girl who steps into a ballet studio, a space Raven claimed for us all, continues her legacy. Through all the hate and rejection she faced, she embodied the famous Bible passage "Love bears all things, believes all things, hopes all things, endures all things. Love never fails. . . . And now these three remain: faith, hope and love. But the greatest of these is love."

And Raven was love.

ACKNOWLEDGMENTS

The world is a better place having had Raven Wilkinson in it, so writing this book was an incredible honor, and I'm so grateful for all who contributed to it.

Steve Troha, thank you for your brilliant book ideas and for helping make them a reality. Gretchen Young, thank you for believing in me and this book and helping make it what it is.

Candace Itow and Eleanor D'Antuono, your voices added so much beautiful texture to Raven's story. Thank you for your candor and openness. I know Raven is smiling down on us.

Olu—my husband, my best friend, and my rock—thank you for holding me and our one-week-old son down while I finished the manuscript.

Gilda Squire, your work, love, and guidance stretch far beyond being my manager, and your beautiful relationship with Raven helped to bring this book to life. Thank you for your contributions and unending support.

Susan Fales-Hill, I can't imagine writing this book with anyone else. Thank you for going on this journey with me and for helping tell Raven's and my story in a unique and powerful way.

NOTES

Chapter 3

1. "Intersections: Conversations on Arts and Culture," Misty Copeland, Raven Wilkinson, and moderator Brenda Dixon Gottschild, Studio Museum in Harlem, May 12, 2011.
2. Wikipedia, s.v. "Dunbar Apartments," last modified March 29, 2021, https://en.wikipedia.org/wiki/Dunbar_Apartments.
3. Raven Wilkinson, interview by Jack Anderson, 1977, New York Public Library for the Performing Arts.
4. Wilkinson, interview.
5. *Classic Black: The Experience of the Black Dancer in Choosing a School,* film, 1996, New York Public Library for the Performing Arts.

Chapter 4

1. Allen, Zita. "Raven Wilkinson, Ballet Pioneer and Mentor to Misty Copeland Passes at 83," *Amsterdam News*, January 10, 2019.
2. Margaret Fuhrer, "Raven Wilkinson's Extraordinary Life: An Exclusive Interview," *Pointe* magazine, June 1, 2014.
3. Raven Wilkinson, interview by Jack Anderson, 1977, New York Public Library for the Performing Arts.
4. Wilkinson, interview.
5. Raven Wilkinson clippings, New York Public Library for the Performing Arts.
6. Wilkinson, interview.
7. Wilkinson, interview.
8. Eleanor D'Antuono, in discussion with the author, February 4, 2022.

Chapter 5

1. Eleanor D'Antuono, in discussion with the author, February 4, 2022.
2. Raven Wilkinson, interview by Jack Anderson, 1977, New York Public Library for the Performing Arts.
3. Wilkinson, interview.

Chapter 6

1. Raven Wilkinson clippings, New York Public Library for the Performing Arts.
2. Wilkinson clippings.
3. Margery Beddow, "If It's Tuesday, I Must Be with the Ballet Russe," *Dance* magazine, November 1991, Wilkinson clippings.
4. Raven Wilkinson, interview by Jack Anderson, 1977, New York Public Library for the Performing Arts.
5. Wilkinson, interview.
6. Eleanor D'Antuono, in discussion with the author, February 4, 2022.
7. Wilkinson, interview.
8. Wilkinson, interview.
9. Wilkinson, interview.
10. Wilkinson, interview.
11. Wilkinson, interview.
12. Wilkinson, interview.

Chapter 8

1. Margaret Fuhrer, "Raven Wilkinson's Extraordinary Life: An Exclusive Interview," *Pointe* magazine, June 1, 2014.

Chapter 10

1. Jennifer Dunning, "Sylvester Campbell, 59, a Pioneer among Black Classical Dancers," *New York Times,* April 6, 1997.

Chapter 13

1. Candace Itow, personal phone interview by the author, April 11, 2022.
2. Itow, interview.

INDEX

A

ABT's Studio Company, 18
Ailey, Alvin, 8
Alek Wek, 33–34
American Ballet Theatre (ABT), 3,
    8, 30, 37, 45, 46, 56, 146, 148
Ananiashvili, Nina, 19
Anderson, Lauren, 86–87
Anderson, Marian, 8
Anne James Wilkinson (Raven's
    mother), 41
Anxiety of black parents, 7

B

Balanchine, George, 20, 29, 204
A Ballerina's Tale, 109
Ballet Russe de Monte Carlo, 6, 8,
    61, 125
Ballet Society, 20
Ballets Russes, 17, 19
Bells toll
    completely elasted and ready for
        vacation, 176
    loved God, family and ballet, 179
    promotion to principal dancer,
        175
    Raven's kindness, 179
BET Nightly News, 24

Beverly Bond, 127
Black Girls Rock, 127
Black Lives Matter movement, 208
Black Nureyev, 170
Blatant racism, 206–207
Bradley, Cynthia, 128
The Bright Stream, 39, 48
Brisbane, Australia, 131
Browder *v.*, Gayle decision, 91
Brown Jackson, Ketanji, 3, 4, 8
Brown *v.* the Board of Education, 91

C

Café Luxembourg, 48, 103
Casting: Princess Florine, 52
Chicago Defender, 63
Christopher (Chris), 102
Cinderella, 163
City Center auditorium, 43
Colorism, 32
Coppélia, 122
Cornejo, Herman, 205

D

Dabney, Stephanie, 79
Danilova, Alexandra, 42
Davis. Viola, 8
Denham, Sergei, 57, 61

Direct racism, 211
Discrimination in dance, 5
Dixon Gottschild, Brenda, 28, 33
Don Quixote, 19
Dreams realized
 a big hug with a little brown girl,
 162–163
 company meeting to review, 164
 dozens of journalists peppered
 with questions, 165
 growing profile and positive
 reviews, 161
 stepped outside the theatre and
 crowd cheered, 162
 thankful speech, 162
Dryad Queen, 110
Du Bois, W.E.B., 42
Dutch National Ballet, 171

E
Equality in dance, 213

F
Favorite snack, 2
Ferri, Alessandra, 19
Ferri, Fabrizio, 81
Firebird, 78–80, 82, 84–87, 102, 125
 character, 134
 DTH's world-renowned signature
 pieces, 79
 girls and boys carrying their
 copies of book, 162
 performance, 83
Floyd, George, 2
Franklin, Freddie, 20, 23, 24, 42, 62

G
Gamzatti, 76–77
 humanity and not a "mean girl"
 interpretation, 77

George, Nelson (Film director),
 85
Gilda, 15, 24, 25, 33, 79, 102, 126,
 182, 184, 185, 192–193
Giselle, 18, 48, 66, 67, 69, 71, 183,
 184, 211
Gomes, Marcelo, 48

H
Hallberg, David (ballet superstar),
 48, 204
Harlem Renaissance, 41
Haywood, Claire H., 5
Herrera, Paloma, 19, 48
Hoffmann, E. T. A., 42

J
Jamison, Judith, 8
Jimenez, Tai, 79
Joffrey Ballet company, 31
Johnson, Christina, 79
Johnson, Louis, 29
Jones, Doris W., 5
Jones-Haywood Dance School,
 5
Jones, Paunika, 79

K
Kirov State Academic Theatre
 of Opera and Ballet. *See*
 Mariinsky Theatre
Kniasef, Boris, 105
Ku Klux Klan, 96, 114

L
La Bayadère, 19, 76, 83
LaBelle, Patti, 126
Lady of the Camellias, 47
Le Corsaire, 109, 110
Les Sylphides, 27, 71, 94, 113

Life in Motion, 102, 162
Loring, Eugene, 31
Losing the religion
    dancers apologized for their foul
      language, 169
    devote yourself a body and soul,
      168
    lived in Chelsea called the
      Carmelite sisters, 168
    moved to Wisconsin and lived
      among nuns, 167–168
    Raven missed America and her
      family, 171
    Raven's longevity surrounded
      with friends, 172
    Sylvester Campbell stayed in
      Europe, 171–172
    woman of deep faith, 167
Lyric Theater, 131

M
Madame Swoboda, 43, 44, 56
Makarova, Natalia, 19, 84
Mariinsky Theatre, 76, 148
Metropolitan Opera House, 37, 52,
    135, 144
Mitchell, Arthur, 4
Motley, Baker, 8
Murphy, Gillian, 48

N
Nelson, George, 107
New York City Ballet (NYCB), 20,
    29, 119
New York City Opera, 40
New York's *Amsterdam News*, 63
No longer together due to
    COVID-19, 208
Novak, Nina, 115
The Nutcracker, 66, 69, 70, 104

O
Odette/Odile, 87, 125, 133–135
O'Malley, Martin (Surgeon),
    100–101
Opera House, 62

P
Pennsylvania Ballet, 119
Petipa, Marius, 52–53, 148
Pointe magazine, 144
Promise of possibility, 8

Q
Queensland Performing Arts
    Center, 131, 132

R
Ratmansky, Alexei, 39, 48
Raven Wilkinson, Anne, 23, 24, 28
    advice and feedback, 48
    as ambassador of United States to
      Cuba, 68
    artistic life, 42
    ballet jokes, 104
    battle between body and mind,
      150
    battling within myself, 67
    to be a proud Black woman, 81
    black ballerina generational
      trauma, 135
    body rejecting to lead, 137
    on bus trip to an engagement in
      Philadelphia, 115
    career-ending injury, 107
    celebrated for talent as a dancer,
      113
    Chris closing the email, 104–105
    Chris love letter to Raven,
      103–104
    and Christopher (Chris), 102

Raven Wilkinson, Anne, (*Cont.*)
  colorism, 32
  Columbia University student, 44
  a cup of coffee in coffee shop, 97
  Dalcroze method, 43
  dancers pay respects, 34
  diagnosed with COPD disease, 182
  doctor advice, 99
  Eleanor's admiration for Raven,
    65
  emotional and economic
    uncertainty, 36
  exquisite feet of, 65
  fate of Black dance prodigies, 30
  found Inogen to breathe, 184
  fractures in the tibia, 99
  frustrations that Black ballet
    dancers feel, 31–32
  future potential, 44
  gentle manner and infinite
    patience, 49
  getting ready for rehearsal,
    133–136
  Gilda and, 25
  greater obstacles of, 64
  historic meaning of career, 124
  humiliations, 95
  irreverent humor, 28
  "the least I could do was try," 58
  love and support in everything,
    182
  loved God, family and ballet, 179
  member of ABT's corps de ballet,
    72
  member of corps de ballet, 72
  nagging doubts, 146–147
  needed a portable oxygen tank,
    184
  Nelson came with idea of film
    with Raven, 107
  not a burden or pressure, 8
  and Olu, 35, 37
  "one-step forward two-steps
    back," 9
  Prince Siegfried's love at first
    sight, 134
  promise of possibility, 8
  returned stage at Brooklyn
    Academy of music, 107
  revolutionary exercise technique,
    105
  Screwing metal plate into exterior
    tibia, 101
  screws to support six stress
    fractures, 107–108
  thanksgiving, 181
  unexpected consequence of
    injury, 101
  when one door closes another
    opens, 102
  working privately with teacher, 121
Robbins, Jerome, 29
Robeson, Paul, 42
Rockfeller, John D., 42
Romeo and Juliet, 18, 19
Roosevelt, Franklin Delano, 41
Ross, Tracee Ellis, 8
Rothbart, Von, 134–135
Royal Academy of Dance (RAD),
  204
Robinson, Bill "Bojangles," 42

S
Saunders, Kellye, 79
Scheherazade, 66
Second-class citizenship, 4
Segerstrom Center for Performing
  Arts, 182
Silence does not bring about
  change, 210–211

Sims, Anne Benna, 5, 18
Sleeping Beauty, 52, 109–110
Studio Museum (Harlem), 17, 27
Swan Lake, 18, 19, 52, 66, 108, 109, 125, 131–133, 135, 152, 204
Swoboda School, 56

T
Tallchief, Maria, 20
These Three, 31
Thirteen Diversions, 77
Trailblazer: The Story of Ballerina Raven Wilkinson, 183

V
Vaganova technique, 148, 204

Verbal and physical brutality against black people, 6–7

W
Washington, Kerry, 8
Wheeldon, Christopher, 77
    Firebird Casting, 78
    intricate footwork and intense passion, 77
    Thirteen Diversions, 77
    won Tony award for best choreography, 77
Wilkinson Frost Birnie (Raven's Father), 41
Williams, Camilla, 8
Wolf Trap National Park, 205

ABOUT THE AUTHOR

Misty Copeland is a principal dancer at American Ballet Theatre and the author of the *New York Times* bestsellers *Life in Motion, Ballerina Body, Black Ballerinas,* and the children's picture book *Bunheads,* as well as the award-winning children's book *Firebird.* She made her Broadway debut in 2015's *On the Town,* putting the show into the Broadway box office top ten for the two weeks that she guest starred as Ivy Smith. She's been featured in the *New York Times* and on *CBS Sunday Morning* and *60 Minutes,* and she was named one of *Glamour*'s Women of the Year and *Time* magazine's 100 most influential people. Misty is the recipient of the Young, Gifted & Black Honor at the Black Girls Rock! Awards and the Spingarn Medal, the NAACP's highest honor.